You Just D

You Just Don't Listen

A parent's guide to improving communication with young people

Suzie Hayman

VERMILION
London

1 3 5 7 9 10 8 6 4 2

Text © Suzie Hayman 1998
Text illustration © Peter Cox 1998

First published in the United Kingdom in 1998 by Vermilion
an imprint of Ebury Press
Random House
20 Vauxhall Bridge Road
London SW1V 2SA

Random House Australia (Pty) Limited
20 Alfred Street, Milsons Point, Sydney,
New South Wales 2061, Australia

Random House New Zealand Limited
18 Poland Road, Glenfield,
Auckland 10, New Zealand

Random House South Africa (Pty) Limited
Endulini, 5A Jubilee Road,
Parktown 2193, South Africa

Random House UK Limited Reg. No. 954009

A CIP catalogue record for this book is available
from the British Library

ISBN: 0 09 181653 X

Cover design Slatter Anderson

Printed and bound in Great Britain by
Mackays of Chatham plc, Kent

Acknowledgements

I'd like to express my warmest thanks to all the young people and parents who made this book possible. You are all too numerous to mention, but you do know who you are!

Special thanks have to go to my husband Vic and our young person, Alex – who between them taught me how to be Good Enough.

Contents

Introduction

Have you got a sullen and rebellious teenager who says that you simply don't understand? Do you and your children seem to have nothing to say to each other – or have all too much to say, but none of it makes sense? I've been there – in fact, everybody who has ever had a teenager in the house has been there. Which means it's highly unlikely that the reasons for your difficulties are that you are a uniquely incompetent parent or that your youngsters are uniquely awful adolescents. The problems you may be having are the outcome of the situation, not the individuals. Your teenagers are growing up, and that's the reason for your troubles. That doesn't mean, however, that any difficulties you and they may be experiencing with your relationship are fixed and constant. You can change, your teenagers can change and the situation can change – it just needs a little communication. *You Just Don't Listen* is here to open the lines and make talking to each other not just possible, but fun. Read on, and within a few short months you could find:

- No more fights (just creative discussions)
- No more mess (well, not in the living room or where it gets in your way)
- No more late nights or 'forgotten' homework (without prior agreement, that is)
- No more tearing your hair out over your children's manners, clothing, friends or make-up (you may even get a taste for purple highlights and pierced eyebrows!).

You Just Don't Listen will:

- Help parents and children communicate with each other and understand each other's point of view
- Build bridges between the generations by building up your and their self-esteem
- Encourage their respect for you – and yours for them
- Fill you in on all the tricks of the trade of being an effective parent.

As parents, we all too often have very high expectations of ourselves. We all want to be the perfect parent – caring, knowledgeable and in charge. The reality is often very different. We usually flounder around in a welter of self-recrimination, believing ourselves to be incompetent, incapable and stupid. Parents' disappointments at their 'failures' often spill over into anger and frustration that may be taken out on the children as well as themselves. Difficulties in understanding and getting in touch with our teenagers are often at the centre of our doubts about our ability to be good parents. One of the most destructive myths that causes these problems is that being a Mum or Dad and knowing how to communicate with our young people, are somehow instinctive arts that we are all born with.

> Parenting and communicating are skills that we all
> have to learn

On the contrary, parenting and communicating are skills that we have to learn. *You Just Don't Listen* is a book about these skills and how to acquire them. I hope to help you identify and feel confident in what you already know, and to recognise the areas that you might like to strengthen or change. The book looks at how to detect the trigger points, the moments when a situation may be getting out of control, and discusses how to increase your skills in avoiding or making the best of these. But the accent will be on doing it yourself. While other people can help you in your job of being a parent, you are the ones rightfully in the driving seat. You should be the ones able to pick and choose and make the decisions as to how best to bring up your own children. My main aim is to stress the fun that can be had of living and learning with teenagers, and how to make it far more enjoyable, constructive and energising.

We often ask for help with the tricky questions we expect to hear from our children – 'Why can't I have a motor bike?', 'What's wrong with smoking?', 'Can I go on the Pill?'. *You Just Don't Listen* outlines the range of subjects your teenagers might like you to discuss and offers ideas on how you might approach these. The main aim, however, is to consider, practise and feel comfortable with the basics of communication. Once you become a parent who is 'askable'; that is, happy to be approached by and seen to be at ease with talking to your children, the rest falls into place. The key is to be effective, whether using complex or simple language or no language at all, and effectiveness comes out of self-confidence.

Becoming an 'askable' parent is the goal

You Just Don't Listen is for anyone, whatever your sex or gender, whether bringing up children as part of a couple, on your own, or in an extended group. Many of the skills we need and use while parenting are common to men and women and are interchangeable. Mother figures need to be tough just as much as father figures need to know how to hug, kiss and shed a few tears. And you don't have to be blood related to be a parent-figure or to parent.

Central to my main argument is a discussion of parenting styles. 'Parenting styles' aren't simply a matter of the current fashion of how we think we should bring up our kids. They're about the choices we make – or find out

have been made for us – in dealing with our youngsters.
In the good old days when 'Men were Men, and Women
were Women', the authoritarian style was thought to be
the best method of bringing up a family. Adults were in
charge and children did what they were told. Discipline
seemed to be the main focus in any discussion about
parenting – the more it was used, the better you were
said to be as a parent. When Dr Spock (not the one with
the pointy ears) came along, the boot seemed to pass to
the other foot. Now, in some American families, where
parents have adopted a liberal style, the children appear
to be the ones calling the shots.

Parental types

Most of us fall into one of eight broad categories or
parental/family types when it comes to being parents.
Whether we realise it or not, we follow a system or set of
rules that lie behind the way we may approach and deal
with different situations. You may find you identify with
at least one of these.

- Some people are 'Do as you're told' parents. Rules are
  important in such a family and are pretty inflexible.
  When there are disagreements, they are usually ended
  by Mum or Dad putting their foot down.

- Others are 'No rules at all' parents. Anything goes and
  what is acceptable and not acceptable can change
  from day to day.

- Then there are the 'We've got troubles of our own'
  parents. They are so overwhelmed by their own troubles that they have very little time or attention left over
  to engage with their children.

- Another variation is the 'Family secrets' relationship.
  In this, there are certain things, from the early days of

the family in question, or going way back into their past, that they can't or won't talk about. The result is that there are plenty of other subjects that can't be discussed openly, such as emotions or sex.

- A further example is the 'Angry' parents. These are couples who might both have had so many bad things happen to them in their lives that they constantly seem ready to hit out and blame everything and everyone around them. These feelings spill over and affect their whole family life.

- The 'Anxious' parent is another type. They love their children and their partners and want desperately to do their best as spouse and parent but have no self-confidence in their ability to be either.

- Yet another group is the 'Do it for me' parents. There were so many things they wanted to do when they were young that somehow never happened that now they put immense pressure on their own children to live their lives for them.

- And, last of all, there are the parents who do seem to have got it about right. They are 'Good enough' parents – not perfect, not saintly but comfortable, confident and loving. Good enough parents can have moments of being any of the above. But the key to their families is listening and discussing.

Most of us parent with a mixture of those styles, mixing and matching day by day. I get an enormous number of letters to my agony page from parents. What most people want – and what I wanted when our boy was a teenager – was:

- To be reassured you aren't the only one having difficulties
- To know your anxieties are normal
- To have practical suggestions, to help you communicate better

- To hear how other people made a difference
- To see that any efforts you make will work.

We hope to be good parents, to bring our children up with a sense of purpose but, most of all, with the knowledge that we loved and cared for them. We want to do right by them, and to this end I hope *You Just Don't Listen* will give you some ideas on being 'Good enough'. On a personal note, I can assure you that I've tried and now use all the suggestions I make on the following pages – as do many of the parents I've spoken to. They work, I promise you!

Chapter 1
Why talk?

'Parenting is a very important profession; but no test of fitness for it is ever imposed in the interests of the children.'

George Bernard Shaw

'Talk to your children' may seem a pretty superfluous and rather impertinent thing for an outsider to say to you. It's a bit like being told to breathe or eat. For heaven's sakes, we do it all the time – don't we? Sadly, the truth is that we talk with our kids far less than we think we do. Research shows that most parents spend an average of eight minutes a day talking to their children. Cast your mind back over today, yesterday or last week and try to focus on what really happened between you and your children throughout one day and at specific points in each day. With your hand on your heart, how often can you say you sat down and had a real honest-to-goodness conversation with them? For most of us, a great deal of family interaction is done on the run, with rapid-fire instructions, questions and statements. At a few seconds for each, it actually adds up to very little. More importantly, that's not what communication – a conversation – is really all about. In most child/parent interactions, the reality is that we talk **to** our children or **at** our children and very seldom **with** our children. What distinguishes genuine communication, whether you call it discussion, conversation or just a damn good chunter, from any other form of interaction is that it is genuinely two-way. Communication is when you listen as much as talk, when you hear as much as be heard, when taking in the other person's point of view is just as important as putting your own ideas across. Communication is an exchange of ideas, not a transmission of instructions.

We can often get stuck in futile disagreements with our kids that never seem to come to an end or a resolution. No argument is as bad as the repetitive argument that goes nowhere, where you feel the other person isn't listening to you, or where one or both of you feel the other is simply nagging. If you find this is happening between you and your teens, that would be one very good reason to revisit and review the way you communicate with each other. It's more than likely that all of you could benefit from brushing up on your communication skills. However hostile the atmosphere may seem, or stuck you feel, there are ways of calling a halt to the process and of putting these old arguments to rest.

Change can be hard work – but worth it

The prospect of changing the way you and your family get on may seem much like hard work. If you are experiencing problems, it's often tempting to think it will all resolve itself someday soon – and that poking and prying at the situation may make it a lot worse. If that is how you feel, consider this: what is the very worst scenario you can imagine in your family? Continued arguments, perpetual disagreements, sustained hostility? Whatever your predicament at the moment, the fact is that by doing nothing, you are probably encouraging your fears to materialise. By taking action, however painful, you could have the opportunity to direct matters. Taking the initiative is at the core of any happy family. Don't listen to the myths that say tinkering with it only makes it worse. That may be true of clockwork; not of relationships! There are a number of practical actions you could take that might contribute to a stress-free family.

It is, however, all very well saying that communication is essential and that we should all talk to our children more. But how do we do that? The trouble is that being able to communicate effectively is not an art we are born with but a skill we need to learn. For something so important it's an appalling fact that most of us have had very little chance of learning how to do it confidently, easily or expertly. We don't learn to do so at school, and often we don't learn communication skills from our parents. The downside of this is that if you are having difficulties, communication skills may be something you will have to get, practise and perfect as an adult. The upside is that it means you are not alone in missing out, and it's not your fault that you may need to brush up on these abilities. Most important of all, it also means that it's never too late to learn.

What's so special about communication?

So, what's so special about communication? Communication is not just a question of getting people to listen to you, it has to be two-way. If you want somebody to hear what you are saying you have to offer them the exchange of listening to what they are saying. Many people think making themselves understood is the same as getting their own way, and this may be one reason we sometimes refuse to listen to the other person's side of the argument. We think that if we do hear them out, the chances are they might 'win'. But proper communication doesn't lead to just one person's ideas being taken on wholesale. On the contrary, it leads to negotiation where everyone has their say and is heard and a final solution is found that satisfies everybody to some extent. An important point to note is that after negotiation you may not get precisely what you want, but because everyone gets part of what they want you are all encouraged to go along with the final decision.

Communication has to be two-way

As a parent, it may seem on the surface and initially that
you can get a lot more done, and with less fuss and trouble, if you are in charge. If you operate from the standpoint that you have the power and the authority it might
appear that there are not going to be endless discussions
or arguments.

Leonie and Duane feel that rules are important in a
family. She says:

❝Our three are always trying it on and simple things, like getting them all up and ready for school in the morning, can
be a nightmare. They used to be difficult enough when they
were all young but now the eldest is a teenager, she can be
such a pain. If Duane wasn't there putting his foot down, I
don't know what would happen. But it can get so tiring
because she seems to get worse. Every little thing is the
excuse for an argument or a disagreement. My sister says we
should let her go her own way a bit more or do it differently. But if she takes any excuse to give us backchat now, think
how difficult she'd be if we invited it! ❞

Leonie and Duane, who are 'Do as you're told' parents,
feel that standing firm and applying the same rules and
expectations as they formed when their children were
tiny is the line of least resistance. Some parents may feel
that exactly the opposite is true. Small kids may do what
they are told or you may be able to force them to do so,
but when it's a teenager you're dealing with there will
come the day when the balance of power may shift.
Sometime, they may look you eye-to-eye and recognise
that when push comes to shove you will not be able to
enforce your demands. This may be the main reason why
learning communication skills is so essential for the
parents of teenagers. Asking them to do something, and
talking it through with them, is simply a more effective

way of dealing with them than trying to insist and enforce.

> communication is more effective than force

If what you want to build is a better way of dealing with your teenagers, communication is the foundation. If you are wondering how this may work and how you might introduce it to the young people in your own family, let me reassure you that research on the subject suggests that most young people easily grasp the concept of communication and all that goes with it. They recognise the importance of a two-way flow and know what makes it succeed or fail. Although they may be resistant to any early attempts – and this is discussed at a later point together with ways of dealing with it – the main opposition may not be from them but from us, the adults. We are the ones who may find most difficulty in adapting to a new and different style of parenting.

Talking with, rather than telling, as a parental style means you listen and learn instead of simply pontificating. Even disagreements with a bolshy teenager can be defused with understanding and humour.

Striking the balance

It can be hard to strike the balance between giving guidance to young children, and letting older children make decisions for themselves. A lot of what we expect child/parent interaction to be about actually stops proper communication. When we become parents we assume that we have a function – to produce Good Children. To be a Good Parent we think that means that we should be competent and in control and that we need to be this at all times. It's difficult to have a meeting of minds when your continual assumption is that you know best. This, in turn, suggests that you don't have to listen or take on board the other person's point of view because they have nothing you need to hear. This may work with young children, although to be frank I have my doubts even about that, but there can be absolutely no doubt that if this is your parenting style you are likely to run into problems when you try to apply it to teenagers. Power-play parenting tends to lead to arguments, sullenness, defiance and a stubborn refusal to co-operate. It's exhausting and such a waste of time, not only because you have to swim against the tide all the time but also because you have to think of everything.

If you're 'in charge', you have to do all the work

As adults and parents, we frequently make decisions we think are best for our children, because the result seems right. We choose where we're all going on holiday, where we're going to live, what schools they will attend and sometimes even what subjects they will study. You may feel this makes sense, because they seem to be in agreement. And how many times have you said, 'Oh, we're doing so-and-so again – you liked that', to be stunned by the reply, 'No, I didn't.' The usual response would be to argue, to tell them that they'd got it wrong and you had remembered correctly.

Are teenagers 'children'?

But why do we continue to treat, and think of, hulking great teenagers as small children? One reason may be that childhood has been made to last longer in the twentieth century than in any age before us and longest of all in the last decade of the twentieth century. Up until the latter half of the nineteenth century you would either be a child or you would be an adult. There was very little in between and you'd move from one state to the other fairly rapidly. Childhood was a time of physical and emotional immaturity when you were wholly dependent on your parents. The taking on of an adult role tended to coincide with the development of a mature body. Of course, some children may have been expected to work and take their place in the adult world, but at the other end of the scale very few people with an adult's body did not expect to do so.

One of the key changes in the latter half of the twentieth century has been that the transitional phase between childhood and adulthood has gradually lengthened and a whole new state of being has been established. Adolescence or the teenage state is now accepted as a wholly distinct time of life. During adolescence young people may acquire physical and emotional maturity but still, politically, financially and legally, be considered to be children. That is, dependent upon and under the control of their parents or carers. However, we do see adolescence as a transitional phase – a bridge between childhood and adulthood. The problem with this is that we don't accept adolescence as a state in itself. We spend our entire time telling our kids and ourselves that this is an undesirable and uncomfortable interlude through which you need to hurry. Instead of allowing them and us to enjoy it for itself we build up a level of discomfort and anxiety about where they are, what they are and who they are. We concentrate so much on the future rather than the present and spend so much effort hurrying through that we forget to enjoy it as it is. Since it's an 'in between', a 'neither/nor' that is, in effect, only a staging post between two stable states, we also tend to see it only as a dysfunctional and problematic condition.

> Two-way communication makes parenting
> so much more fun

If parenting more effectively is the primary reason for communicating with your children, another is that two-way communication makes parenting so much more fun! One sad aspect of parenting during the teenage years is that it seems for many people to turn in to something of a marathon. The expectation is that this is a period that is inevitably difficult and therefore has to be 'got through'. This expectation is often self-fulfilling. The period in life when your kids are at their most energetic, exploratory and exciting, when the entire family can be swept along by their freshness and enthusiasm so often becomes simply a battlefield that gives pleasure to no one, least of all them.

Adolescence – the risks and the pleasures

We tend to place too much emphasis on the dangers surrounding the teenage years: the difficulties of adolescence, the evils of peer pressure, the decline of the family. Get parents together and what do we discuss? The horror stories. We talk about our teenagers' awful friends, the risks they run from drugs and dangerous driving, the fear of ill-considered and premature sexual activity with the hazards of pregnancy and sexual infections. Just as we all roll, with relish, in the tabloid headlines about burglary and road rage it's all the negative aspects we dwell on, not the pleasures. We look back with longing on a fabled Golden Age of childhood and wonder what became of our little angels.

Diane and her partner Eddie noticed the way conversations with all their friends seemed to take a turn for the worse over the last year or so.

6Whenever we'd meet over a meal or for a drink, we'd always end up talking about the latest murder or rape in the news. Then someone always starts in on swapping stories about their kids and just how ill-mannered and uncontrollable they'd become. Sooner or later they're telling anyone who's got kids still at primary school that just you wait, it'll get you too! Ours are 10 and 11 and I'm just all wound up, expecting them to turn into Frankenstein's monster any day now! **9**

Good parent/child relations, however, do not deteriorate just because your child suddenly hits the brick wall of double figures, puberty and adolescence. That parents and teenagers argue isn't the problem. Any relationship, if it is close and dynamic, rather than distant and static, will encounter differences of opinion. Any family members or firm friends who love and are committed to each other but who are not robots lacking a mind of their own will have disagreements. It's why and how you argue that matters. A difference of opinion during which all parties feel their point of view is being heard and shared and where everyone comes away with their dignity intact is a learning experience that can be enjoyable. In families this is often not the way it happens.

> That parents and teenagers argue isn't the problem, it's why and how you argue that matters

What often does change in the young people concerned is that they do start thinking for themselves and want to make their own way, and for many of us this throws up all sorts of uncomfortable feelings. Although parents are neither at fault nor to blame when families find themselves stuck in a futile cycle of arguments that get nowhere, we do have to take responsibility for what happens in our families. 'Fault' and 'blame' are not helpful concepts. They are judgmental statements which imply a level of wilful stupidity or malice. If we think something is our fault we feel guilty about it and when we feel guilty we get angry. When we get angry we are often inclined to refuse to look at what is happening or why and to modify the situation. When you accept responsibility, change is within your power. Perhaps the most important aspect of parenting is to recognise that becoming a parent doesn't in itself endow you with skills, just power – for good or bad.

We seem to have quite conflicting beliefs about parenthood in our society. On the one hand we give it enormous status, priding ourselves in being parents. Ask most people what was the high point of their lives, the most important thing they had ever done or the part of their life that they would least like to be without, and most would say it's having their children. Yet, on the other hand, we give parents very little actual practical support and help. Nowhere is this more obvious than in the way we prepare people for parenthood, or rather fail to prepare them. When we talk about parenting, many of us, somewhat self-defensively, claim it's really all common sense. But, as Giambattista Vico (1688–1744), Italian philosopher and historian, said, somewhat wryly:

❝Common sense is judgement without reflection, shared by an entire class, an entire nation or the entire human race. ❞

Common sense simply isn't enough to get you through the very difficult and complex tasks of bringing up children from their birth to their adulthood. You aren't born with the skills for parenting. The impulse to love and care for other people and the need to have them love and care for you maybe inherent, but the ability to do it well has to be learned. The question of course is; where and how do we learn this craft?

Although more and more schools are seeing parentcraft as being an essential subject that should be covered by them, most of us who have children at present have not benefited from any formal discussion. We tend to have picked up our expertise at home from our own parents who, in turn, learned from theirs. What they learned and taught is frequently the problem and this is discussed in more depth later on.

Effective parenting

Communication is the glue that binds together all the various skills of parenting. When I talk about being an effective parent I'm not simply talking about ways of ensuring your children do what you want them to do. This is often seen as the most desirable goal – of having kids who behave in ways you find desirable and do so without argument or complaint. Most of us would realise that obedient children, while making for the quiet life, are probably not exactly a natural, normal or in any way attainable achievement. But we do tend to feel that if only we knew the right buttons to push or the right things to say we could persuade them round to our way of thinking and that, surely, would be a 'good thing'. But communication is not about persuasion, or only about getting your ideas across. It's about listening as well. Teenagers frequently complain that their parents don't understand them, and parents even more often bemoan the fact that teenagers don't listen, don't agree with and don't care about manners, morals or your hopes for their future. They may know about your particular moral system and your hopes and expectations for them. They simply may not share them.

Communication is not about persuasion, it's about agreement

As parents we are always delighted when our children take their first steps. Those emotions are second only to the pride and delight you feel when your child utters their first word. We may feel concern at the possibility of their stumbling or falling, but we know that they have to experience the odd bruise to make it on their own. And we know, above all, that they do have to stand alone to develop into healthy and strong individuals. It's strange, then, that we so often have mixed feelings when our kids start learning to stand on their own two feet in other ways. What we are doing, throughout their lives, is trying to help them build the competence and confidence to grasp independence. It isn't, however, always easy to let go and allow them their freedom, and this often shows itself in the way we act towards young people and their behaviour. Talking **with**, not **at** or **to**, your young people is a vital part of building a system that will work for you and work for them.

The Horse Whisperer

I recently watched a television programme featuring a Horse Whisperer – an amazing man who, instead of breaking horses, tamed them with kindness. He was showing and passing on some of his skills to a young woman who had been riding all her life. In the short space of 20 minutes she had a previously 'wild' horse following her round the paddock and she was reduced to tears because she had never before had the experience of a horse wanting to be with her in quite such a trusting fashion. Instead of breaking the animal and making it do what he wanted by force and willpower, this man enlisted the animal into a consensus, an alliance. He befriended the horse, by acting with it the way one of its own fellows would behave. As I watched, his performance brought together all I had felt about the relationship we so often have with the creatures that share our lives – our children and other young people. We frequently see them as animals, members of another species that we have the responsibility to bring to heel and civilise. Like most animal tamers, we take the view that the best and most efficient way of doing so is by making the exercise a contest of determination and strength. Maybe we should follow the example of the Horse Whisperer.

The keys to successful communication

There are three keys to successful communication: respect, unconditional love and flexibility.

Respect

Respect is a buzz word when it comes to child/adult relationships. Politicians are forever bemoaning the state of

---

Exercise: **negative and positive statements**

There are a few honourable exceptions but, in my experience, our beliefs about parenting and children tend to fall into either negativity or sentimentality. Sit down with your partner, take paper and pencil and list all the statements and beliefs you might have heard about children and parenting – all the clever sayings and little family jokes that you find yourself coming out with when you think of your teenagers and being a parent. Here are a few examples:

Children should be seen and not heard
Spare the rod and spoil the child
Slugs and snails and puppy dog tails – that's what little boys are made of
Sugar and spice and all things nice – that's what little girls are made of
Give them an inch and they'll take a mile
A small child is a noise surrounded by dirt
Insanity is inherited; you get it from your kids
Children are an investment in the future.

Once you've got the list, divide the statements into two; those that are positive, enthusiastic and kind about children and parenting and those that cast it in a negative light. See which is the bigger list and which are the stronger, more memorable statements. Discuss with your partner and your young people how this might affect your attitude to being a parent.

---

the youth of today, saying they have no respect for society. Adults often complain that kids show no respect for their elders and betters and parents frequently worry about the lack of respect they feel their children have for them. What tends to be missed in such complaints is that respect is actually two-way. To get it you need to earn it, and to earn it you often have to give it. Children often fail to learn to respect their parents because they catch on pretty early that their parents often have difficulties in respecting them. This is hardly surprising when you consider many of the messages we take on board about children and parenting.

Significantly, both negativity and sentimentality bear a remarkable resemblance. As the renowned child psychoanalyst Donald Winnicot once said, 'Sentimentality is repressed hatred.' This isn't to say that we hate our children, but we do often have extremely angry feelings about childhood that express themselves in these unproductive beliefs and expressions and which affect the way we do the job. Why we have them and what they are all about is looked into later. But being sentimental about childhood and children means we distance them from ourselves – we make them a special group and a special category. This means that we treat them differently – and differently doesn't always mean nicely. If you want to know whether you are treating another person with respect, or whether they are treating you with respect, there is one and only one test; ask yourself, 'Is this the way I would want to be treated?' Would you like and expect your partner to treat you the way you treat your teens?

Unconditional love

We all need to have our efforts and abilities praised, rewarded and valued. But even more important is to know that we are loved, respected and valued simply in ourselves. Anyone, but most of all young people, flourishes best when the people they love and value make the effort to tell them, firmly and frequently, that they are valued and loved too. We call this unconditional love. When you only give praise when a young person has done something – in effect, you praise the result not the person – they can't help feeling that they are only valued when they perform, and perform well. When a young person knows you value them, they have every incentive to listen, attend to and rate what you might have to say to them.

Flexibility

We tend to put a value on consistency in parenting – on saying what we mean and meaning what we say and sticking to the same line, time after time. This is all very fine but there are occasions when you need to know how to walk the tightrope between consistency and rigidity. With a young child you may be able to say they can or can't and have it your way. With a teenager, you don't have that power. Negotiation is the name of the game. Whatever the subject – sex, drugs, drinking – you may find putting your foot down simply doesn't work, and it's a choice between your bending or breaking. True communication means going into a discussion with a firm idea of what you want to say, but an open mind on what you might hear and what all of you might end up deciding.

Self-control

Talking to young people can help you become a better, more effective parent. It does this, not by persuading your youngsters to do what you want, but by enlisting them into doing what is best for all of you. If discipline and safety are issues that concern you, the simple truth is that with teens, self-control is the often the only control you can rely on. If you want them to be safe and socialised, the best tack is to build up their self-esteem, self-confidence, self-acceptance and self-appreciation rather than their obedience. One child-care expert explained it as follows:

❝While criticism or fear of punishment may restrain us from doing wrong, it does not make us wish to do right. Disregarding this simple fact is the great error into which parents and educators fall when they rely on these negative means of correction. The only effective discipline is self dis-cipline, motivated by the inner desire to act meritoriously in order to do well in one's own eyes, according to one's own values, so that one may feel good about oneself – may have a "good conscience". It is based on values which we have internalised because we have loved, admired and wanted to emulate people who lived by them – for it is in this way we hope ourselves to be esteemed by these significant others. It is not much of a conscience which tells us not to do wrong because we might be punished. The effective conscience motivates us to do right because we know otherwise we will suffer all the pain and depression of feeling bad about our-selves. In the last analysis, we will reliably do right only in order to prevent the pangs of conscience – to feel good about ourselves, not to avoid punishment. ❞

Bruno Bettleheim *A Good Enough Parent*

Young people are often convinced that they are perform-ing for an audience. They live in a permanent agony of self-consciousness, convinced that every blush and stam-mer, every hesitation and stumble, is under scrutiny and the subject of other people's scorn and derision. One reason for this self-centredness is purely physical. Their bodies are surprising them with unexpected, rapid change and growth which is often confusing and even frightening. They can't help becoming clumsy and awk-ward as they struggle to manage limbs that have grown and a centre of balance that has probably shifted. But another reason is that it isn't arrogance for them to be convinced that they are constantly being overlooked when the truth is that frequently they are. We don't allow teenagers to have their own points of view, to trust their impulses, interpretations or self-image. We tell them we're right and they're wrong, imposing our own view of and on everything so they can only see themselves through our eyes. It's hardly surprising, therefore, they see themselves constantly through other eyes.

Bad behaviour

Why do young people behave badly – and what do we mean when we say 'bad behaviour'? Children who shout, children who run around making a noise, children who ask repetitive questions may all be labelled as behaving badly – as displaying 'Attention-getting behaviour'. 'Oh, s/he's only trying to get attention' is a phrase we may hear, or use, frequently as children grow up. I've heard it used of toddlers tugging at their parents sleeves, asking them to look, listen and talk to them. I've heard it of children slamming doors, fleeing the kitchen when they've been told for the fourth time, 'Stop interrupting, I can't come and look now, can't you see I'm cooking dinner?' I've heard it said of teenagers who drink too much and drive too fast, and of young people on their second or third suicide attempt. In a culture that still feels emotions are messy and frightening, and children should be seen and not heard, we seem very quick to label any demands on the part of young people to be heard as BAD. Why not look at this another way? What appears as bad behaviour is often a recurring attempt on a young person's part to get their needs met – needs that are not selfish, unreasonable or impertinent but natural and normal.

When young people are 'bad' there is always a reason. Teens who are lazy, unmotivated, rude, uninterested are usually so because:

- Low self-esteem means they feel 'I can't' rather than 'I can'
- They feel nobody is really noticing them
- They're scared of failing and feel it's safer not to try
- Too high standards or expectations mean they feel they can never please
- Too low standards or expectations mean they aren't being stretched
- They're under pressure from peers not to achieve
- They have an undiagnosed/untreated problem – such as dyslexia.

Negative thinking, about young people in general or your own teens in particular, begets negativity. If we start off from the foundation of believing that what they think and what they do is a problem, or is in any way undesirable, we're looking for obstacles rather than solutions. What then happens in our relationship with them, and their relationships with others, is usually a result of how we respond to this frame of mind. Communication with our young people is the first step in getting away from a negative frame of mind, and from the problems this so often creates.

Families and democracies

There is another, and to my mind the most important, reason why we should communicate with our children. When you talk to them, and listen too, you make the move from running your family on paternalistic 'What I say goes' lines towards building a small democracy. We spend a lot of time in this culture lambasting communities around the world who do not, we think, have fair political systems under which everyone can enjoy freedom and human rights. Yet, if truth be told, we hardly run our own families under the conditions we'd like all communities to be run. If we can say that it is fair and right for people to be able to stand up for their own con-victions, to have free speech and a say in how they are ruled, to live free from fear and to have independence, at what point do children become people? One reason that so many societies are still dictatorships – and the rea-son the trains tend to run on time under a fascist state – is that they can be far less complex to run. You have to expend a lot of wasted energy keeping down rebellion, but that aside, it can be simpler. And, of course, it means that the people at the top have the immense satisfaction of being in control and having first pick of the goodies. A family is the same. And for the same reason as we in this society stand up for human rights and dignity and accept some of the extra work, fuss and bother that goes to make a democracy, I vote for participatory families, too.

Exercise: **Self-identity**

Take a moment to look at this picture. In your role as parent, with which figure do you most identify yourself?

Were you sitting at the top, calling out to your children down below? Were you hanging on by your fingernails, or were you one of the group walking along the top? How you saw yourself in this picture should give you some clues as to how you view parenting and your particular performance of the task.

If you see yourself as just clinging on, it might be pretty obvious that you view yourself as not doing too well. If you were the person striding out in front, you could say you feel in control and content. But does being a leader make you a part of your family or an outsider?

The place you picked, however, may not be one that an outsider can interpret for you. The point of this exercise is for you to choose the spot that seems to describe how you feel, and to consider and talk over why that may be the one that calls to you. Once you can understand how you feel about parenting at the moment, you will then be able to pinpoint the aspects you might like to change or rethink.

The main answer to the question 'Why talk?' is that it will make your life, and your children's, easier and more pleasant. It will help you move from paternalism to partnership. To move, that is, from the parenting style that puts you in the position of always having to come up with the answers and to be the one pushing from behind – which can be very tiring – or leading from the front, which makes you quite a target for stray bullets. You may find parenting a whole lot more fun if you can see it, not as an arduous task where you are rolling a massive rock uphill, nor as a dangerous encounter where you are leading your troops into battle. Parenting should be a romp and stroll in the countryside with each member of the family leading and following on occasion, but most of the time where you and your children go side by side.

Shelley and her husband Mark saw a counsellor because of problems with their marriage and with their two children 11-year-old Matt and 16-year-old Steven. Shelley particularly felt that she was no good as a mother and said that as long as she could remember she knew she was, 'No good at most things'.

Both she and Mark felt so overwhelmed by their own problems that they had little energy left over to cope with their children. Shelley's self-esteem was very low. When asked about her own family and upbringing she insisted that she had had a happy childhood with loving parents who cared for her. She spoke particularly warmly about her father who she said had a good sense of humour. After several weeks of discussion she started talking about teasing and it emerged that her father made heavy use of sarcasm with all his children and was particularly prone to, 'Put me in my place. You know, put me down when he thought I was getting too big for my boots.' Getting too big for her boots seemed to mean whenever Shelley ventured an opinion or made a request. Shelley herself at first claimed sarcasm was a form of humour that everybody used and that, as her father had said, her sense of humour got her used to 'the rough and tumble of real life'. She and Mark used it frequently with their children. But the more she talked, the more the tears flowed. Gradually Shelley was able to admit to herself that this 'humour' had been immensely hurtful. It soon became clear it had resulted in her feelings of low self-worth, and had much to do with the difficulties she and Mark were having with Matt and Steven.

One reason for talking is for your young people's sake, to make their teenage years pleasanter and more productive. But you should equally do it for yourself. Perhaps you have lingering hurts and resentments over the way your own parents managed your adolescence, maybe you feel – as many people do – that you could have been listened to, heard and respected a little bit more. You can't go back and rewrite the past. But, by yourself being the parent you might have wished you had, you can repair some of those disappointments. While doing it for your kids, you can also do it for yourself.

To a certain extent, parenting requires you to be pretty selfless in many ways. Once you've taken on the responsibility of bringing other lives into the world you can't always put your needs first and always have to take theirs into account. But there is a balance to be achieved. Parents who sacrifice their all for their children can end up being miserable themselves. They also actually produce children with an unbalanced view of relationships. Part of listening to another person in the way that allows them to have their needs met by you is requiring them to listen to you too. It's an important aspect of development for no one in the family to miss out either in being satisfied or in having the experience of learning that you can't have it all every time. 'Selfishness' is actually a necessary and helpful trait, at the right time, in the right place, and in the right doses.

It is never too late to change

It is never too late to change the way you do things, either with your family or your partner. What often holds us back is not the difficulty in identifying where change is needed or in managing it, but the fear of change, and of losing control. We're scared that seeing how and why we may want something different might cause us to look back and feel pain or anger at the wasted, lost time of doing it in the old way. We're scared that a new regime may put us on the spot and we won't be comfortable or competent at managing it.

Making changes

Any group of people who are in contact with each other will have arguments and disagreements from time to time – families more than most! When there are teenagers in the family, you may find the atmosphere can steadily deteriorate with arguments that appear more bitter, longer and harder to resolve than the little spats you had with small children around. You may feel that the problems are your fault for not trying harder or the young person's fault for being so unreasonable. In effect, you may well feel that the people in this situation are to blame. If you are going to make the situation better, there are three steps you can take that will carry you towards a solution.

- The first is to EXPLORE – to look at what is happening in yourself and in those around you
- The second is to UNDERSTAND – to see why you feel and act the way you do and what you might do about it
- The third is to ACT – to make changes in your responses and behaviour to bring about the arrangement you would like.

Exploration, understanding and action are the three stages of change that counsellors use to help an individual, couple or family transform a problem into a solution. None of them work in isolation. Just talking about a situation hardly helps on its own. Achieving understanding isn't like being given a magic wand. Just because you know why you feel and act the way you do, doesn't mean to say that everything will automatically be better or easier, although it does help. And rushing around without first seeing what you are doing and why may give the impression of improving matters without actually changing anything. Once the dust has settled, everyone returns to being the way they were.

In this society there tends to be a lot of resistance to talking about emotions and motives, to exploring and understanding. When you're having problems that might have started in your own childhood, wondering and trying to work out why is often thought of as raking over painful ashes. This is a bit like believing that you should leave well alone if you cut yourself. If you have a painful wound it is often tempting just to slap a plaster on and do nothing else, because opening up and cleaning the area would hurt so much. Of course, if that is what you did, the wound would fester and the end result would be far more dangerous and painful. Emotional wounds act in exactly the same way. It is only by facing up to what has happened that we can heal them and avoid repeating the same mistakes. If you stick your head in the sand like an ostrich and hope nobody can see you, what is actually going to happen is that you will probably get run over! As a counsellor, I've seen that 'raking over' the distant and immediate past can only help you make a better future. The idea of this book is to give practical suggestions on how you can come to terms with your feelings, discuss them with the rest of your family, get support from those around you and make changes. The techniques of discussion, negotiation and compromise can help anyone, even argumentative teenagers, take responsibility to make a family work.

It is often hard to change because of the common belief that if something goes wrong somebody must be 'to blame'. Most of us grow up with a nagging feeling that we don't quite come up to scratch and feel we could always have done better. Young people in particular are very quick to believe that their parents are faultless and that they are always in the wrong. You may have been lucky enough to have grown up in a family with people who helped you to feel good about yourself, where you were praised for doing things well more than you were blamed for doing things badly, and you would have become someone who valued her or himself. If you were not, the chances are you would have grown up with a tendency to think it was your fault when things go wrong. When we think we're in the wrong, it's a very human reaction to point the finger at someone else as quickly, and as loudly, as possible. This is why, when young people are at the stage in their lives when they long to prove their competency, they can so easily feel lacking and so quickly lose their tempers. And we feel on edge and touchy, too, because watching them go through this stage throws us straight back into vivid memories of our own teenage angst. The next section looks at what may be stopping us communicate with our teenagers, before looking at ways of overcoming those barriers.

Chapter 2
What stops you talking

They fuck you up, your Mum and Dad.
They may not mean to, but they do.
They fill you with the faults they had
And add some extra, just for you.

Philip Larkin

If it is difficult to really get down to communicating with
our young people, what is it that stops us doing so? Some
things actively hinder our getting in touch; others don't
exactly help us. But before we can make changes so that
we can talk more easily, it helps to understand what may
be holding us back.

Perhaps the most important barrier to communication
is simply the fact that we may not have learned how.
Parenting isn't instinctive. It's not a skill we are born with
but an art we learn. If you find this hard to believe,
ponder the study made on a group of monkeys that had
been removed from their parents at birth. The scientists
doing the research made sure they were nourished properly but they were never held or cuddled, as they would
have been if brought up by their parents. In short, they
were never 'mothered'. When they, in turn, had young of
their own, they hadn't the vaguest idea of how to treat
their offspring and were distant and neglectful. The
drives to need and seek love, sex and food may be
inbred, but how we actually ask for or deliver those
things we have to learn. How we parent, we learn from
our own parents.

How do we learn to parent?

How we were brought up affects the way we can and do relate to our children, in several important ways. The way our parents behaved to us can affect our parenting style. Our beliefs about when children should go to bed, whether the family should all sit down for an evening meal together, what constitutes 'cheek' and what is normal give and take, all have their origins in our own childhood. But it's not just the nuts and bolts of how we behave as parents, and expect our children to act, that we copy from what went before. We also have demonstrated to us how parents and children relate to each other, and we see emotions either made legitimate and acceptable, or made taboo. We may learn that parents hug and kiss you, or are seldom there when you really need them. We may learn that a parent drops everything when you need to talk, or always tells you to wait because they are busy. We may learn that parents can be loving, but they can also be angry and hurtful to children; or that anger is so frightening that it is never allowed to be expressed.

If we come away from our own families feeling that our childhood experiences could be improved upon, we have one, big problem with putting this into action. Most of us have a good idea of what we did like and what we didn't like, how we would and how we wouldn't want to be. But at the same time few of us have a reliable blueprint for knowing how to do it differently from the way we were brought up ourselves. Our own parents are our role models and even if we don't like what they did, we find ourselves falling into and following the patterns they set and taught us by example.

> We learn to be parents from our own parents whether we like their way of doing it or not

In longing to be The Perfect Parent, our expectations of ourselves, and indeed of our children, are often unrealistically high. But not knowing how to do it means our anger and disappointment can be equally disproportionate. The real problem, of course, is in coming to an understanding of what may be holding us back, how and why.

There is an ancient oriental proverb that says 'The fish does not understand the water it swims in'. From the outside looking in you may see that other families bring up their children in a different way than you do yours. It would be possible to recognise how their behaviour is dissimilar, and perhaps to understand where this results from beliefs and attitudes, and how it affects each person in the family. It's often very difficult to do the same to our own. In effect, the way you live your life just 'is'. You can't necessarily see the strings or recognise the unconscious principles that underpin your way of doing things. It can be quite difficult and quite uncomfortable trying to examine what you do and why. But it can be done, by asking yourself questions and facing up to the answers. If you are not entirely happy with the way your family is going, understanding your own parenting style would be the first step to seeing how this may be helping or hindering you and your family. Once you've done that you can go on to choosing a better way of doing it.

Understanding your own parenting style

We tend to operate from a range of beliefs about parenting which affect the way we act to our teenagers. 'Mother knows best' is one, 'Don't talk back to your parents' is another. Neither are helpful to communication between you and your teenager. One refutes the need for discussion, since there's no point in talking if one of you can never learn and therefore never needs to listen to the other. The other stops conversation dead since it implies that the first time you hear anything you don't instantly like, you'll use your authority to shut them up. You won't know how to parent positively if your parenting was essentially negative. Negative parenting is parenting by prohibition. It's when you are told off for doing wrong but never praised for doing right. It's when you are punished for being bad but never rewarded for being good. It's when you can always guarantee having attention paid to you when you are misbehaving but know you will be ignored when you are being good. There are other forms of negative parenting, however, that actually appear to be loving and helpful. It may be easy to see how constantly telling a child he or she is wrong, bad or stupid will demoralise them and lead to a loss of self-confidence or self-esteem. But telling them 'do' just as much as we tell them 'don't' can actually be as stifling and dis-empowering.

> 'Do this . . .' stops young people learning for themselves just as much as 'Don't do that . . .'

It's very easy to fall into the trap of directive parenting. We tend to feel as adults that we know best. We tend to feel that it's a sad and dangerous world out there and that we would love to protect our children from danger and from making mistakes. We see our job therefore as passing on the benefits of our own experience and of guiding and protecting them. We can find ourselves issuing a steady stream of instructions, suggestions, cajolery and commands: 'Do it like this . . .', 'Why don't you do that? . . .', 'Wouldn't it be a good idea if you? . . .', 'I'm sure it would be best if you . . .'.

We can all cite examples where our help could be seen to be essential. OK, maybe we could have bitten our lip and let a toddler spend an hour working out a way of building a stable tower out of those play bricks, but wasn't it better to show him how? And surely it was just common sense to tell her how to carry a full cup across the kitchen floor, otherwise she'd be sure to have spilt it. Doesn't it make sense to instruct a child how best to ride a bike, to inform a teenager what exams he should be taking, to tell them they mustn't do this and shouldn't do that? It's common sense to let her know why she mustn't take drugs, why he oughtn't to hang out with those kids down the block and why that particular article of clothing is a very bad idea indeed. After all . . . Mother Knows Best! But cast your mind for a moment to your own teenage years. What sort of things did your parents tell you that you might have disagreed with? What did you think when they said them? And, more important, what did you feel?

> To be a Good Enough Parent of a teenager it helps to remember what it felt like being that age yourself!

The problem with 'dos' is that they prevent a child from exploring and discovering and building competency. It's difficult to become experienced in solving a problem if you never have the chance to try it out for yourself. It's particularly difficult if you are forever having demonstrated to you the fact that you don't know how to do it and somebody else does. What tends to happen is that even though you learn the trick of putting brick on brick, you learn at the same time that you had to be told how. You don't learn the satisfaction and the confidence that comes from making a mistake and learning from it, not only how to complete the particular task at hand but the lesson that you can do it, eventually. Young people need to be allowed to try out new skills in safety, with our expectation that they are trustworthy, they can succeed and that a mistake isn't such a terrible thing. When teenagers fling out of the house loudly announcing that they don't care what you think and that they are going to do it their own way, it's often because they know from long experience that not only do you not trust them but that they are not trustworthy. In a desperate attempt to prove to you and to themselves that they can do it, they will often fail purely because they haven't been given a chance to practise acquiring new skills on their own, without a constant stream of instructions and criticism. Inevitably, something will go wrong and they'll carry onwards the conviction that they are no good.

We learn best when allowed to make our own mistakes

The Interfer-iority complex

What most parents have is an Interfer-iority complex. We feel that we have to guide, instruct, inform, to do our job properly. You'd probably never dream of spying on friends, colleagues or relatives – or if you did, you'd feel a bit shamefaced, knowing interfering in someone else's life in this way is unethical. But many parents think reading their teenagers' diaries, listening in to phone calls, speaking to teachers or other involved people behind their backs and without their permission is perfectly defensible. After all, we reason, it's 'for their own good'. We feel it's part of our role as a parent to make them feel better, to solve their problems, to know what they should be doing. So when we feel that our young people have a dilemma, we rush in with our fix, providing what we think they want or need, regardless of even strong messages to the contrary. Needless to say, the response we meet is often hostile or impatient, and can result in our teens being even less willing to open up to us.

Anna, an anxious parent, feels she tries hard to do her best for her children:

❝All I ever seem to hear is "Oh, Muuum!" It's amazing how much scorn and contempt a 15-year-old can put into two words! And I can't see what I'm doing wrong. I do try. I know they're both having a tough time at school – Josh has his GCSE exams coming up and Toni will be choosing her subjects for hers soon. So I've tried to come up with suggestions that could help but it seems everything I say they reject. It's funny, but when Josh was born I was so happy. I wasn't much good at school myself and the job I have is pretty ordinary. I thought that at least I would be good mother. But it seems I've failed in that as well. **'**

Seeing parenting as a job where you are in charge gives you a vested interest in feeling you can solve any difficulties experienced by your young people. We tend to think the inexperience of young people is the same as their not being competent or capable. Standing by and letting them find their own solutions may leave you feeling anxious and angry and incompetent. We make it a source of pride that we know best and decide for them. This means we are upset and angry when they complain or resist our help or direction.

Coming up with the quick fix

It also means we may resort to making light of their fears and anxieties if we fear we can't come up with the quick fix. We may be dismissive or over-reassuring, discounting their own feelings or experience. We often feel it's part of our role to tell them how they should be feeling: 'There, there, it's not as bad as all that!', 'You should be happy', 'You can't still be hungry!'. Sometimes this is because they and we really do have conflicting feelings at that moment and we're trying to make them come around to our point of view. But sometimes, we ourselves are in the same state as them but we don't want to acknowledge it and we try to persuade them to come round to how we think we and they should be feeling.

We may have what seem to us to be good reasons for plainly flying in the face of our teens' expressed feelings. We fear that by acknowledging negative feelings without correcting them we'll reinforce their anxieties. So when a teenager cries out 'Everyone hates me!' we think denying this is the best method for making them feel better. In fact, doing this only tells them not to trust their own feelings and not to trust us.

> The style many of us adopt is of constantly correcting or directing. Even before the words say anything our manner towards them tells them we don't feel they can manage for themselves.

By offering our own interpretation of what is wrong and what is needed, we discount their own needs and their own ideas. Young people and parents often find that what stops them talking is parental intervention, and this takes one of three forms.

Judging

When parents are quick to sum up and be judgmental about what their youngsters have done, to blame and criticise them, they may feel there is little point in talking to you. It may be obvious that putting anyone down doesn't help them do better, it only makes them feel inadequate and incompetent. But what many people don't realise is that even less harsh ways of summing up a young person can reinforce feelings of hopelessness and failure, and make them want to avoid, not seek, discussion with you.

Playing the expert

Forever diagnosing your youngsters' actions or feelings and coming up with solutions can make them feel powerless and incapable. You're bigger, more experienced and capable – why should they ever try to do it for themselves? And why should they bring problems to you, when all that will happen is that they'll end up feeling worse?

Diverting

Parents often feel a reassuring way of dealing with their teens' dilemmas is to change the subject, telling them to 'Cheer up, it doesn't matter'. But far from diverting their minds from the difficulty and making it go away, this method leaves the young person feeling discounted and unvalued, just as their worry was discounted and unvalued.

Personal experiences

Our own experiences of what passes for communication may not have been beneficial, and may not have left us with positive feelings about talking and sharing. Paula says:

❝A saying I was brought up with was "Those that ask, don't get". That's such a horrible thing to say to a child. I suppose it stops, or is meant to stop, all those whining "gimme" type of arguments, but to me it says a lot more than being demanding is unattractive. It stopped me at a very young age from trusting my mother or wanting to tell her what I thought. I can always remember the one time I said, "But if I don't tell you what I want, how do you know?" She told me not to be so cheeky, she was my Mother, of course she knew what was best for me. I'd had enough of being told off already that day, so I didn't point out that what I wanted and what she thought was best may not be the same. I knew from that moment that my feelings were never going to be something she was interested in hearing about. The terrible thing is that I have to admit I have said it to my children, when they've been getting on my nerves. Only a couple of times, though. I remembered where I'd heard it and how it made me feel. ❞

Exercise: communication blocks

It's surprising how many proverbs and old sayings there are that discourage us from communicating with each other. Here are a few, but how many others, either common or personal to your family, can you think of?

Least said soonest mended
Those that ask don't get
Silence is golden
Curiosity killed the cat
Children should be seen and not heard
What you don't know, can't hurt you

Discuss with a trusted adult – and, perhaps, with your teenagers – how this may have affected the way you communicate.

The beginning of the end

The teenage years are the time when we finally have to acknowledge that the birth cord has been cut. It's the beginning of the end as far as hands-on parenting is concerned, and that makes it a time of reflection and often apprehension. Once they grow up, they can begin to judge you – and you may feel nervous at that prospect. Once they leave, they can choose whether or not and when to come back, and that may alarm you. Once you are on your own, you may be scared you'll find there is little left in your life if you are no longer a full-time parent, and that can be terrifying. All in all, there are plenty of motives for you to stand in the way of progress.

When you were young, you may well have had times when you and your parents were not seeing eye to eye and you said to yourself, 'When I'm a parent, I won't do it this way.' Once you're in the situation, you find yourself doing exactly what they did, with exactly the same results. Why does this happen? Why is it so hard at times to deal with your children, to love them or enjoy them, or treat them well?

Exercise: why did you have kids?

How do you think your reasons for wanting or having children might affect the relationship you have with them? If the pregnancy was unplanned, you might always have felt that they were an unexpected gift and value their company. But if you felt their very existence prevented you from experiences or achievements you may otherwise have had, you could resent them and be quick to find fault. If you had a child to find someone who would love you, you might feel frightened at any conflict or angry that being a parent meant more give than take. If you had children to gain a sense of achievement and usefulness, you might view the prospect of their growing up and becoming independent with alarm as it makes you redundant. Have a look at the reasons some parents have given to that question, below. Tick the ones that ring a bell with you, and add your own. They might give you some clues as to what is behind your feelings towards your children, yourself as a parent and the job of parenting. Consider the ways they might affect your relationship with your children.

Everyone has kids
You're less of a man/woman if you don't
To have someone to look after me in old age
To have a stake in the future
To have someone to love me
To feel wanted
To feel useful
I was under pressure to produce grandchildren
It was an accident!
I wanted to have a baby.

> Unfinished business from our childhood affects the way
> we relate to our children

We've begun to consider how difficulties in communicating with your teens may come about because communicating is a skill we need to learn, and we may miss out on gaining it at home or at school. There is, however, another barrier that could come between us and our kids. Unfinished business from your childhood can affect your parenting as well. If your parents behaved towards you in ways that you found confusing, dissatisfying, painful or frightening, you may believe that your main aim would be not to pass that on to your own children. Children whose parents often hit them will frequently say they are determined never to hit their own kids. Parents who grew up in homes where sex was a taboo subject often say they will talk freely to their own children, when the time comes. In the event, they find it harder than they thought.

One reason is that, whatever they did to you, you love your parents. We are always drawn to forgive, to protect and to explain their behaviour and the reasons for it. We often follow in their footsteps as a way of legitimising their actions. By adopting them yourself, you tell yourself, and your Dad and Mum, that the way they brought you up must have been acceptable and right. You reassure yourself, and them, that you know they loved you and that you emerged unscathed. But there is another, sadder and darker, reason for adopting a parenting style or pattern of behaviour that caused you pain. Anna's ex-husband Brian is a firm believer in discipline. He says:

> I was hit regularly by my father and it never did me any harm. It taught me a valuable lesson. I was a tear-away and he did it because he loved me to try and get me to toe the line. I respected him for it. He was hard but fair and he never hit me unless I deserved it, which I did most days. In

fact, sometimes he hit me and said I'd probably been up to something and here was one just in case. He was usually right! I want my kids to grow up like me, knowing right from wrong, so Anna and I disagree on this. She says you should never hit kids but I think she doesn't realise what little devils they can be if you don't keep a firm line. **'**

When children find themselves at the receiving end of parental discipline it can be frightening and overwhelming. Whether the child is simply being told off or the extreme of being beaten and all points in between, the child may feel a profound sense of powerlessness. The adult is bigger, stronger and has all the resources. The child can feel overwhelmed with a sense of helplessness and hopelessness and overwhelmed also by anger and even hatred. These are profoundly uncomfortable feelings and as well as wanting the telling off or the beating to stop, the child will very much want these uncomfortable feelings to go away too. In a lot of ways the strength of the emotions occasioned by the behaviour of their parents may be more frightening, painful and uncomfortable than the punishment itself. Feeling powerless and out of control is probably the worst of all and that may be the emotion that children most want to get rid of. This is often why children will be happy to accept the idea that if they were punished it was because they deserved it.

For a start, it's always more comfortable to believe that your parents, whom you love and on whom you depend, are fair. If you have to say that they punished you for no good reason, you are having to face the fact that all is not right with the world. That is a very scary prospect for a child. To accept the rightness of your parent's actions is to believe, at least, in justice and consistency. Further, if you say that you deserved your punishment you are also taking on yourself a measure of control over it. In other words, it wasn't arbitrary or out of your control, it was something you almost chose and invited. When a child grows up you would again think that if they had received punishment they didn't enjoy they would not want to pass this on to their own children in turn. But if it was the feelings of powerlessness that were the most painful and difficult, the feelings of gaining control will be experienced as a resolution and cure.

Faced with your child doing the sort of things you got punished for you may find yourself drawn to reclaim the old scene but this time with yourself as the one in control. You will banish that horrible feeling of fear and powerlessness, by playing out the scenario with a different ending, this time with you calling the shots. And every time your child does something that reminds you of yourself in a similar position you may find yourself reaching yet again for this method of drowning out those memories.

Labels

Good labels can be as harmful as bad ones. Either way they get you stuck in a role that may not be appropriate or that you may not want to fulfil. When we label people rather than behaviour, we fix them in that particular pattern. If you say to your teenager that they are lazy, rather than that they are behaving in a lazy manner, you effectively tell them that that's the way they are, period. In the same breath as saying it's not something you like, you actually imply that it's not something they can change – it's not something they are doing it's something they are. When you tell yourself you are useless or incompetent or no good, you fix yourself in being like that and give yourself no hope of making any change.

If you don't want your child to behave in ways that upset you, the first step is to start looking at those unattractive aspects as behaviour rather than the person.

Not that they are selfish but that they are behaving in a selfish way. Not that they are unhelpful, but that they are being unhelpful at this particular moment. Not that they are inconsiderate but that that was an inconsiderate thing to do or say. If you don't label yourself, you can choose to stop labelling your child. And if you stop labelling your child you will have taken a first step towards changing the things you don't like them doing.

We all put labels on ourselves, and on others: 'Sheila? Oh, she's always been the joker in our family', or 'You're just like your Uncle Fred, he was a rebel too.' Sometimes the labels seem complimentary: 'Who's Mummy's little helper?', or 'He's such a good child, never gives me any bother.' Sometimes they can be more damaging: 'Your father was a no-good and you'll end up like just him.'

Exercise: **negative and positive beliefs**

Your own self-image and your feelings (or lack of them) of self-worth will affect the way you parent your children. It's very easy to label the young people in our families and for us, having acquired a label, to accept it and grow up with it. Indeed, we often grow into labels, because once you've been told you are the joker, the black sheep or the stubborn one in your family you may as well act that way because it's hard getting anyone to see you as different. Take this opportunity to list the beliefs you have about yourself, as an individual, a parent and a partner. For every negative belief – I'm no good at organising, I'm lazy, I'm a useless cook – fill in something positive – I'm loyal, I'm funny, I don't give up easily.

Now you have filled in your lists, sit down and think about and discuss how, when and why you got these beliefs. Who told you that you were good, who told you that you were bad and why? Were they right, and what have you done to fulfil that expectation and keep that label?

Exercise: **family roles**

Imagine the roles in a family being like a set of fancy-dress costumes for a party. Everybody must be dressed in one, whether it's a costume that fits you or not and whether you find it comfortable or not. Once you put your costume on, you're stuck with it. Sometimes you pick your own costume. Sometimes, you find you've had your costume chosen for you. Either way, you may find that even though you want to change later, nobody else can see you in any other set of clothing. And whether the costume suits you or not, as time passes, you grow to fit it.

Look at these words. Can you find descriptions that fit you and your own family? Can you add any more words?

Mother's little helper
Good child
Bad child
Rebel
Tomboy
Joker
Lazy one
Dreamer
Sulker
Little Princess
The little madam
Hard worker
Ne'er do well

Look at the roles occupied by you and your family. Which roles are held by which people? Do you think these people are comfortable in them? Who says they suit their label? Do they really fit? Would you or they prefer not to wear their role? How can you change?

Pain transference

It's very easy to find ourselves lashing out at our kids. They so often touch a raw nerve and we react, telling them off, putting them down, putting them 'in their place'. But how often has that nerve been made raw by something long ago and far away? By a situation, a person, a hurt that is considerably removed from the one you take your anger, fear or pain out on? When teens and parents clash, it's often a case of kicking the cat, transferring a legacy or passing the buck.

Kicking the cat

How often have you found yourself seething with anger from a bad day at work, after visiting friends or family or in the aftermath of essential household chores because of something someone has said or done to you? There's that one final straw and you explode, slamming a door, throwing a mug or kicking poor old Tiger. You may well be annoyed with the someone or something who/which bears the brunt of your anger for something they have or have not done. But the truth of the matter is that your explosion is more to do with what has happened before they came along and triggered it. You are taking out a load of accumulated anger on them and indeed you may find yourself feeling relieved at discharging all that pent-up emotion. It's that relief that can make you feel justified in shouting. You feel better, so it must have been the right thing to do, which encourages you not to enquire further and to do it again next time.

Or you may recognise what you've done and feel guilty, which is just as good a reason to try and seek justification and convince yourself that even if your child was a scapegoat they deserved a telling off anyway. You can then find yourself locked in a cycle of needing to convince yourself that the child you punished deserved, justified or needed that reaction and to go on doing it. What's really going on is that you feel unable to shout at the people with whom you are really angry – your partner, your boss, a relative or some anonymous shop assistant . . .

Transferring a legacy

Because we learn how to parent from our parents we often find ourselves using the techniques, stories and phrases that they used with us. This can be a joyous celebration of family continuity when, for instance, you tell your daughter the story of Cinderella in exactly the same words and in exactly the same circumstances as it was told to you. But when you find yourself shouting 'Because I say so' – a phrase you hated and swore you would never use – it can be less helpful.

What may be even more harmful is that you can find yourself replaying other people's arguments. If there were particular disagreements that came up in your own childhood, the mention of something similar may find you automatically reacting in the way you saw played out in front of you, with you now taking the role of mother and your teen in the position you used to occupy. You will find yourself doing to them what your parents did to you. And the fact that you didn't like it then, instead of preventing you, will actually urge you on. You may feel empowered because this time the shoe is on the other foot.

Passing the buck

Another source of disagreement between parent and teenager can be other people's disagreements with a young person's behaviour or appearance. Conflict may arise because you find yourself under pressure from family, neighbours or the other adults with whom your child comes into contact, such as teachers. You may find your-

Exercise: **what's the trigger?**

We often find ourselves in violent arguments that seem to blow up out of nowhere, and reach astounding levels of aggression. Sometimes, afterwards, we realise our response was out of proportion to the offence but we often feel powerless to understand or stop what happened. This is an exercise to help you work out:

- What makes you angry
- Why it happens
- When it happens.

The question to ask yourself is 'What's the button and what pushes it?' The next time you get angry, sit down afterwards. If talking it over with someone else helps, you might get a friend or your partner to do this exercise with you. Remember what made you angry. Think about when you've felt like that before. What were your feelings when you became angry? What were you doing to deal with those feelings? Did it work? Once you begin to realise your own buttons, and what pushes them, you can begin to deal with them too.

self arguing about the way they look, the friends they have and the things they do because of what the neighbours say or your fear of what they might think, rather than because you actually find it unacceptable. It's not always easy to draw a line between defending your children against outside criticism, when in fact they deserve it, and loading it on them whether they deserve it or not.

Matty hated it when her youngest son, David, left his room in a mess. Every time she went in and his clothes were on the floor or his bed unmade, she found herself becoming sarcastic and bitter, while David got no tidier but became more distant. When Matty did this exercise she realised what pushed her buttons was going into the room and seeing the chaos. She recognised when he did this, she began to feel quite panic-stricken. And when she felt this way, she became angry and blamed David. When she closed her eyes and thought about these feelings, she found herself back in her own bedroom, as a young person. Her mother had been rigorous about tidiness and always made Matty feel totally incapable of doing anything right. However immaculately Matty did keep her room, her mother let her know she was disappointed. Her best was never good enough. The feelings she had when she saw David's room were the same as those she had then – shame, guilt and fear. Her feelings of worthlessness were so great that she became angry, at the person who stirred these uncomfortable feelings in her, David. Matty realised she may have a reason to ask David to keep his room tidy, but her bitterness and anger with him when he didn't were mainly misplaced, leftover emotions from her own childhood. Once she realised WHAT, WHY, WHEN, she found she could cope with the feelings she had and that they became far less destructive.

Getting in touch with your own inner child

As a parent you watch your children taking a journey that you've made before them. At every point in their lives you were once there too. As an adult you are a spectator and an observer of their particular experiences, but the echoes of how you felt, what you did and what happened to you will effect the way you see this. It can effect you in interpreting what you see going on. For instance, you might misjudge your young person's reaction to being asked to be in a school play, thinking they're excited when in fact they are terrified, because it is something you would have loved to have done when you were their age. But memories of our own childhood can effect us in other ways too. Leftover guilt, shame and fear can often prevent us from communicating as we would like. If we were left feeling confused and embarrassed by the way our bodies changed at puberty, it may not just be hard to talk about this to our own teenagers, we may also view their growing up with a mixture of dread and anger as the uncomfortable feelings that we experienced and then buried threaten to overwhelm us once more.

> Get in touch with what was missing for you and you can give it to your teenager

In effect, you need to get in touch with your own inner child. If you can understand what you might have felt was missing from your own childhood you can start dealing with your teenager in the way you would have liked to have been treated, rather than as a result of being in denial about the losses and mistakes of your own childhood. Don't underestimate the role of envy. We would like to be the parents to our children that we wish we had had. But at the same time the angry thought 'I didn't have it, so why should they?' can come between us and them. Paula remembers how this has affected her.

❛When I was nine, I saw a watch in a jeweller's window. Instead of being on a wrist bracelet, it was a tiny, miniaturised watch set on a ring. I fell in love with it and desperately wanted it. In retrospect, it was a tacky gimmick that I probably would have soon have tired of. But at the time I really wanted it. It was near December and I asked my mother how much she would spend on me for Christmas – was it as much, all told, as the cost of the ring, which I seem to remember was just under £20? She said she probably would so I said fine, would she buy me this and I'd be perfectly happy to forgo any other present – no stocking, no books, nothing else but the watch? I was expecting a discussion or an argument. What I got was a screamed tirade, about how she never even had any watch of her own until she was a teenager and certainly not an expensive one until she earned it herself and since she never had anything like that at my age, why should I.

'If she'd said I'd probably regret having only one present at Christmas, or that I'd soon regret having that particular item, we could have talked. I could have understood and maybe sulked, but that would have been that. As it was, over 30 years later I still remember and deeply resent her response. It taught me a lasting lesson. That I was stupid, my request was stupid, my tastes were awful, that there was no point ever asking for anything. After all, if she hadn't had it she wasn't going to give it to me. It taught me that mothering was about competition with your children, that you resent giving them better than you have. Not that one incident, obviously, but I remember it because it crystallised something about my mother.

'Years later, my eldest son once asked me if he could have a jacket I loved but never wore. I said no. I didn't shout at him, there was no argument, but I know he was disappointed. By the time I realised what this was all about, it was too late – he'd grown, the moment had passed. I regret that, although I'll not make the mistake again. In fact, I've since made a real effort to pass on things that mean something to me, something my grandmother loved doing but my mother never did. **'**

The myth of 'spoiling'

Parenthood is bedevilled by the myth of 'spoiling'. Many of us are brought up with dire warnings of the dreadful results of giving in to children's demands, of giving them what they ask for, what they would like and need. The belief is that giving children the 'goodies' somehow teaches them to be more demanding, to get above themselves, to be materialistic and selfish. Perhaps this might be true if what young people mainly demand are objects. But the truth is that money, so often, stands in for something less material. When a young child wants sweets, what they are usually actually asking for is attention. Since from an early age we give them food to show care, the connection is clear. When a teenager demands new trainers, what they often would prefer is time, effort and attention. Giving them as much as possible of that the damages no one.

Parent/young person interaction so often becomes a battle of wills because we feel we know best – and when kids want to do it their way, we feel called upon to defend our corner. Frequently what we are arguing about is not the situation itself but the fact that it's our point of view against theirs. What makes us frightened, and that makes us angry, is the fear that if we give in to them or have to recognise they may be right, it's calling our ability to parent into question. One question perhaps to ask yourself when you and your teenager clash is would you act this way with an adult – and if you did what would it be called? Being abrupt? Being rude? Being pig-headed? Being a bully? What often stops communication is that our teens begin to feel that it simply isn't fair or reasonable for us to demand they work by one standard of behaviour – don't speak out of turn, don't talk back, do as I say, don't be cheeky – while we work to another.

Hand-over time

But there is yet another reason for difficulties in communication between teens and parents, which is that it is actually necessary for them to be able to grow up. The teenage years are a time of transition. As a child, your son or daughter looks to you first. You are the most important person in their life and they want and need to please you. You are their model and their guide and they will listen to what you say – even if it doesn't always feel so! As adults, they will look to themselves. They will have self-confidence and self-discipline and should rely on their own judgements. They may look to a wide range of other people whose opinions they value, including their peers as well as their parents and other older adults, but the chances are that their primary role models will be friends and their partner.

Adolescence is the hand-over time, when they gradually shift the focus from you onto themselves and the people they look up to change from those chosen for them – you and other relatives or carers – to those they choose for themselves. They rebel and don't want to talk to you, not because they necessarily dislike or want to discard your ideas, but because they are testing out what it feels like to be on their own. They rebel because they need to throw your rules overboard in order to try out their own. An orderly passage, where you gradually hand over the reins, may not feel nearly as satisfying as grabbing them.

> Freedom that is given never feels quite the same as freedom that has been won

One way of minimising the effects of this time is to give responsibility and accept that you do need to let them take over for themselves. You also need to accept that they will make mistakes and that this is only to be expected. The main cause of the teenage years being painful, confrontational and angry may not be your rules but a dictatorial use of authority and power. Teenagers in our society occupy a very ambiguous state. No wonder they feel confused:

- At 12, they can't have a job but must pay a full adult air fare
- At 13, they can get a part-time job but can't yet go into a pub
- At 14, they can go into a pub with an adult but having been drinking alcohol for nine years at home still can't have one in public
- At 15, they can be sentenced to youth custody but still not go into a pub on their own
- At 16, they can join the armed forces, buy alcohol, tobacco and fireworks and consent to sex, but not to marriage and they still can't drink alcohol in a pub

- At 17, they can hold a driving licence and be put on probation but they can't vote
- At 18, they can finally (legally) have a drink with friends in their local, give blood, serve on a jury, go into a sex shop and buy a house and vote, but not stand as a member of Parliament or local councillor
- It's not until they are 21 that they are acknowledged as having full adult rights in this society.

With all those contradictions and confusions, is it any wonder teenagers can occasionally be challenging and provocative?

Considering conflict

Of course, arguments can be addictive. If you and your partner, you and your family, find yourself reaching for the familiar of shout, scream and slam every time you have a difference of opinion, it's worth looking at what you might be getting out of it. On one level, you might say or think that nobody has conflicts from choice. That is not necessarily true. There are distinct advantages to carrying on the relationships in your family through the medium of conflict. Do any of these ring true, and can they be forming barriers, preventing you and your young people from speaking to each other?

Payoffs of fighting

- Excitement: every time you have a fight, the adrenaline surges and the spirits rise. An argumentative lifestyle is seldom boring and it can seem a lot more interesting than a calmer, more serene way of behaving. The adrenaline rush can quite literally be addictive and you can find yourself deliberately goading other people into a row or rising to the bait very easily, because you actually crave the physical sensation set off by getting angry or upset.

- Intimacy: an argument can feel a very intimate, close experience. When you are fighting with someone, you can be sharing feelings and secrets you might keep quiet about at other times.

- Distance: arguments, however, control the depth and extent of the intimacy you can have with other people. If you have reasons to fear getting close, you may trigger a row every time you feel you are getting close enough for you to feel vulnerable.

- Strong feelings that seem like love: it's easy to trigger an argument but far harder work to build a loving relationship. Causing a row is a fast track to the expression of strong emotions, which bear a similarity to love.

- Attention: when you're shouting at someone, or they are shouting at you, at least attention is being paid. If you don't trust yourself to be loveable or loving, having a row at least makes some sort of connection.

- It proves they'll stand by you: if you fear that the people you love may leave and abandon you or cease loving you, an argument is a test. If they're still there afterwards, you may feel it's OK.

- It proves you're right in feeling unworthy: if you fear that you're not good enough for the people you love, an argument gives you confirmation that you were right to feel inadequate.

Young people have thoughts, responses and emotions that are every bit as strong and complicated as ours. The problem is that they often find it even harder than we do to understand or deal with their feelings and may hide them better than we do, too. On top of that, young people may find it particularly hard to talk to anyone about their concerns or confusions over the stresses of adolescence. They may be struggling with conflicting and overwhelming emotions but be unable to share them with you, especially if they feel you cannot accept that they have a point of view of their own, and that it will be different to yours.

They have very little real power, only the power of dissent and objection. The only way young people can hit back is by arguing. They can do this with a frightening effectiveness but frequently with very little control or insight into how they really feel and what they are doing. When faced with teenage rebellion, parents often want and ask for help with their behaviour. Children may become sullen and argumentative, have tantrums or become depressed. A frequent reaction is to return to conduct more suited to a much younger child, and to become whiny and clingy, disobedient and rude. Their conduct is often seen as inexplicable, especially when, as is so frequently the case, they may be unwilling or unable to tell you why they are doing this.

Concentrating on stopping the behaviour rather than trying to understand why the teenager behaves in this way will be doomed to failure. If you are to help the young person, you will need to understand how they are feeling and why. Communication and negotiation is likely to require you to accept possibly difficult and uncomfortable conditions. One is that you are going to have to take into account their views and needs.

Signs of stress

The teenage years are an incredibly stressful time. As adults, we tend to see real stress as something we suffer. We look at our worries over earning enough to keep our family afloat, maintaining our relationships, keeping a job, juggling between the needs of various generations, and we feel adolescent anxieties are trivial by comparison. After all, they don't have to keep themselves so what could be so important? We're forgetting that beside the real tasks of adolescence, merely earning your own living is child's play. Teenagers have to decide who they are. They have to acquire the ability to manage responsibility for themselves. They have to grapple with the power, the joy and the desperation of sexual relationships. What's worrying about the fuel bills and the next meal to that?

This is why, when the going gets tough or they need a break, teens so often go back to babyish, disruptive behaviour that you might have thought they had grown out of. They may suddenly revive temper tantrums or behave in a way that demands attention. If they are really feeling unsupported and confused, their behaviour may steadily escalate until it becomes disruptive, destructive and even dangerous.

There's a fine line between the sort of teenage activity that is merely testing the boundaries, and that which has gone over into being beyond the pale. Disruptive behaviour can often be divided into two broad areas – external, where their confusion is being turned against the outside world, and internal, when it is turned inwards. When they are looking outwards, teenagers will pick arguments with their parents and others. If they really don't feel anyone is listening, they may go on to bullying those younger and weaker than themselves, in the family or at school and vandalism. If they're turning their focus inwards and don't feel heard, they may truant from school, do badly at school work or move on to risk-taking such as sleeping around, drug taking or joy-riding. Some children may even turn to self-mutilation, cutting themselves or having tattoos or body piercing from school-friends or professionals. There may be a dramatic contrast in the way they behave inside and outside the home. Some children show their unhappiness by open behaviour only at home and act perfectly normally at school or with other relatives and friends. Some turn it completely around and appear perfectly normal when they are with you but raise hell in school or outside, often to the total surprise and astonishment of their parents when the whistle is blown.

Strange behaviour has a logic of its own and is often a coping technique

---

But disturbed behaviour is not so much a reaction to the changes of the teenage years, as a reaction to not understanding and dealing with what is going on physically and emotionally. However strange, destructive or odd their behaviour, what they are doing is trying to cope with change. In fact, adults practise similar coping techniques when faced with an unstable situation. Young people are particularly adept at putting on an 'It doesn't matter – I don't care' façade. Being cool is important to many teenagers, but refusing to show feelings is more than an adolescent pose. In fact, what young people of all ages often do is to try and cope with anxieties by avoiding thinking about, talking about and facing up to them.

As well as avoidance, young people may deny there is any problem and steadfastly maintain all is well, even when their unease is noticeable. In addition to denial, they are likely to withdraw, becoming silent and non-communicative. Moodiness may be firmly repressed, so the child may appear to be in good spirits, but suffer from tell-tale physical symptoms such as headaches, stomach pains and general ill-health. Children, as well as adults, can also project their feelings, where they externalise or cast out their uncomfortable thoughts onto someone else. The sort of overwhelming, painful feelings so many teens will be having at this time can be too much for them to deal with. Instead of being able to say they are confused or upset, they will want to get rid of these feelings and say they are the target of such feelings from everyone else. It is very hard for a young person to deal with the fact that they feel anger or hate for the people they also love. Hence the impassioned 'You hate me, everyone hates me!' of many an unhappy young person.

The most important fact of all to recognise is that children are separate people, not merely an extension of their parents. They have their own desires but often they need your help in achieving them. Both parents and children can want and need something that is not only different but may be conflicting. Rather than one of you getting what you want and the other one losing out, the trick is to identify what these different things are and then to negotiate towards a position where both can be satisfied.

The *behaviour* may be bad, the *person* isn't

What needs to be remembered is that a young person who behaves in a manner you find unpleasant may not be a 'bad' child, but one who is trying to say something to you. In contrast, a 'good' child, one who is quiet, controlled and obedient, may not be acting in a normal, healthy way at all but be hiding their feelings. Naughtiness and being awkward at least show energy, creativeness, curiosity and LIFE. And 'bad' behaviour may be more in the eyes of the beholder. You may want to label something the child does or says as wicked, not because it is actually wrong, but because it may unwittingly touch a sore point in you. You may have a misunderstanding with a teen and believe they have disobeyed deliberately when in fact they simply don't agree with the rules that you have set and not discussed with them. And sometimes what appears to be naughty or rude behaviour is simply a reasonable response to a changing situation. Just because only one out of several teenagers reacts in a particular way you find awkward, don't think this means they're the problem rather than the situation.

The problem is not the differences of opinion you

might have with your teenagers, but how you handle these; how you approach a disagreement and the person with whom you disagree, and how you resolve a conflict. Often we know it's going wrong but we don't know why or how to change. We feel as if we're on a roller coaster, charging downhill with no way of stopping. We can see that the sort of conflict we're experiencing is uncomfortable and futile, but we have nothing to put in its place.

When you are trying to come to terms with the changing demands of teenagers, it's often important to remember that you have needs too! Anger and impatience with our young people can come about when we feel drained by the demands we feel parenting put upon us. Playing the martyr doesn't only harm them, when they are made to feel guilty about all the things you've done for them or given up for them. Playing the martyr is tiring and painful for the martyrs themselves. But this isn't necessarily because of the demands made on you, but because of the demands you have taken on.

You don't have to be the Perfect Parent

Recognise that you don't have to do it all, you don't have to be the perfect parent and several things happen. For a start, there will be less work to do. You don't have to clean their rooms – if they want to live in disorder in their own territory, that's their lookout. You don't have to run around after them making sure they have clean T-shirts and underwear – if they have to go out dirty enough times, they'll get round to putting used clothing in the laundry basket. You don't have to nag at them to do their homework – if they're going to get in trouble at school that's their lookout. This is not to say that you duck out and leave them to run their own lives. What it does mean is that you negotiate with them ways of allowing them to become self- and internally disciplined instead of needing to be told what to do.

Know when to bend the rules

While consistency is important, flexibility is too. After all, it's the exception that proves the rule. If you are going to be firm about asking for certain things from your young people – keeping common rooms in the house reasonably tidy, going to bed by a sensible hour during the week or doing their share of the chores – being utterly rigid is actually counterproductive. There will be times when you can say 'Hang it' and let them off. You don't have to feel that one relaxation means you can never be firm again.

Being flexible with them also means being forgiving with yourself. While you may be trying hard to respect your young people, to invite them to discuss your decisions and to avoid conflict, you needn't insist on always achieving this aim. Young people do have to learn to take the rough with the smooth. You are allowed to be human – to occasionally be inconsiderate, to sometimes put yourself first and not always to agree with your partner or the other adults involved in your young peoples' upbringing. This also means that you need to accept that young people too are allowed to be less than perfect at times!

Where's Dad?

Communication can be arrested by another unvoiced barrier, which is the absence of men in the emotional life of a family. Mums are, too often, the ones who take care of the emotional life in a family. It's women who cuddle and share loving moments, who read stories to small children, discuss schoolwork and friendships with older ones and are there to talk about worries and concerns as child grows into adolescent. Dad is often absent, if not physically because he's at work or has left the family, then emotionally because feelings are something many men avoid. This gives a powerful message about the legitimacy of emotions and the roles of the sexes. It means that young people find it hard to talk about touchy-feely stuff with their Dads. Which is particularly disastrous when Mum isn't around at the time you may need someone to talk to. And even worse if you happen to be a boy needing to talk about being male – being male, you infer, is about not sharing or expressing emotions.

Exercise: **truth or dare**

Lack of honesty is often a considerable barrier between teens and parents. We can't always be blamed – as we move from one stage of life to the next we often leave behind and forget what we had accepted as normal and suitable to a previous age. If you have ever said 'In my day . . .' or have felt annoyed by something your teen has done or said, try the following exercise.

Make a list of all the situations and subjects over which you and your teenager argue. Here are some, but also add your own:

Drinking alcohol
Smoking tobacco
Smoking cannabis
Taking/using any other substance
Their appearance
Their language or manner
Riding a motor bike
Staying out late
Staying out all night
Their friends
Sexual curiosity/experimentation.

Once you've completed the list, take a long, hard look at it. Write down what age you were when you first did the activities to which you object, or which you worry about with your teens, such as smoking or drinking or sexual exploration. Tick the items that you and your parents disagreed over, such as your friends or appearance. Discuss with your partner whether you think there are differences in the arguments you have now, and had then. Be honest!

Where do we go from here?

What stops us talking, then, are lack of skills, the intrusion of memories and unfinished business from the past. Add to that the fact that most of us are brought up with a negative view of what being a parent, and being a teenager, is all about, and you can see it's hardly surprising most of us find it difficult. The good news is that none of these need continue to stop you. Instead of seeing them as ties that bind, consider them signposts to change. The next section looks at ways of getting started on new methods of talking to our teenagers.

The annual photo

One element that may not be helping your family get on with each other is that you don't share a strong sense of togetherness. Suggest to the whole family that you take a group photo every year, at around the same time and in the same spot in the house, garden or somewhere you can all choose. Acknowledge that there might be the embarrassment of having your photo taken and the horror of seeing, in ten years time, what you thought were cool trendy clothing and hairstyles. But stress that it would certainly please you, and you hope it would please them. You could point out that it would give everyone a laugh to see in ten years time what you all looked like and it would be touching to see the way you grow up together. Most of all, stress it will bring you together as a family.

Chapter 3

Body language and getting started

So you know that communication between you and your teens may be difficult for a number of reasons. It's rarely because of any lack of desire on your part to talk but often due to your inability to begin. By the time your kids are approaching adolescence, barriers may already have gone up to a free atmosphere between you, for reasons looked at in the last chapter. When we are unhappy about being in touch with our young people, we stop communication in a variety of ways. One is through body language.

Body language

When we're not confident and happy as parents, we may find ourselves swinging between submission and aggression. One moment we'll throw up our hands and let them do what they want, just to keep the peace or stop the rows. The next day, we'll come down hard and refuse even the most reasonable request. We often hit out, verbally or physically, because we hurt and we want the other person to do so, too. And the result is that they are diminished and made to feel bad, and so are we.

If you can begin to understand why it may be hard to talk to your teens and what causes these barriers, you can begin to change the situation. The next stage is to understand how your feelings translate into action. How, that

is, you might all have been sending out signals that contribute to or escalate arguments, and how to change this.
Often the main cause of a row is not what we say but how,
when and why we say it.

We pass on as much to our children non-verbally as we
do through language. Research shows that the vast
majority of the information passed on in a face to face
conversation is non-verbal. Only 7% of the impact of any
contact between two people is through their words; 37%
of the message you convey is through your tone of voice.
But a massive 56% is dependant on body language. If we
want to communicate, we need to check out what we are
saying, what we want to say and what we'd rather we
weren't saying in our actions as well as in our words.

The way you stand and the way you speak says far more
than the words you use: check out what you may already
be saying without realising it

Your voice, the way you are standing, the little gestures
you make all have more to say than what you actually
said. When you continue cooking the evening meal/fix-
ing the car/watching television when your teen wants to
talk about something, you say several things. You tell
them you aren't interested in them. You tell them they
are less important than the job in hand. You tell them
their concerns are trivial. You tell them they aren't worth
bothering about.

With body language, goes tone and the way you use
emphasis and language. You can entirely change what
you say and what you mean by altering the tone of how
you say it. A simple question – 'Are you going out?', or
statement – 'I like your hairstyle', can convey anything
from the straight truth of their written meaning, to disgust, anger, criticism. Mixed messages, when the words
say one thing and the tone says another, can be deeply
wounding to anyone, but are particularly hurtful to

teens, struggling as they often are with conflicting demands and desires. The real problem with using sarcasm and other ways of altering a message is that it's dishonest. We use it because we can put a nasty, angry and critical twist to our words, reserving the right to deny what the other person understands by our remark. 'Oh, don't you look a picture!' 'Don't you like the way I look?' 'Did I say that?' The use of sarcasm is probably the one element that teenagers hate most in 'family banter'. The point about give and take, and loving jokes, is that they are only loving if three rules are followed:

- That everyone can give as much as they have to take
- That there is no intent to wound or put down
- That the sarcastic or jokey remark has no hidden message. If you can't say it openly, you shouldn't be saying it this way.

Touchy-feely

Physical closeness between family members – touching, hugging, kissing – says more than just 'I love you'. It also passes on messages of how acceptable, or not, we think we and they are. In some families, parents do find it hard to be demonstrative, especially in this country with its tradition of 'stiff upper lip' standoffishness. It's assumed that everyone knows they're loved, without our needing to go all soppy and touchy-feely to show it. Not so! We need to hear it, to feel it and just because it didn't happen to you, don't assume that means you or your kids should do without it.

Love is . . . always having to say you're sorry

When open affection is withheld, we feel unloved. More important, we feel unlovable and can often assume that the reason for the lack is our own bad behaviour or in-built badness. This can particularly be the case when, as often happens, parents' behaviour to their kids changes when they show signs of entering puberty and becoming sexually mature.

When girls begin to show signs of becoming women, Dads will often change the way they treat them. A father who once played with his little girl, hugged her and paid her attention may suddenly or gradually become critical, punitive and distant. He may withdraw and no longer touch her. Mothers can do the same to their sons when a boy shows signs of becoming a man. It happens because you become aware of their growing sexuality, which might embarrass you. You become aware of how appropriate or otherwise some intimacy may be. Which is fair enough in that you should respect their own decision to draw a line. While children might have welcomed the hug or kiss you want to give, a teen may want to stand on their dignity and only accept approaches they have invited. But your uneasiness with their growth and change passes on a different message, which is that you find it somehow distasteful and worrying.

> You can't spoil kids with too much love, attention or affection

---

What anyone and everyone needs is unconditional, positive regard. You would have liked it when you were young and if it wasn't what you got, you can now bring it into your family by offering it to your children. Unlike a pot of money, an emotional gift does not impoverish the giver. In fact, you've got it, you give it, and you've still got it! Offer it to them and you too get the benefit. Unconditional positive regard is not the same as being totally permissive or *laissez faire*. It doesn't mean accepting what they do, but who and what they are. It means operating from the standpoint that your children are

Exercise: **what do we want?**

We all want to communicate, however angry or unhelpful we may feel or seem. Often, we make repeated attempts and feel, again and again, that it all went wrong. If you took the time to consider what happens and why, you could identify what helps, and what hinders you and your young people talking to each other.

Sit down with your children round a table. Ask someone to do the writing and give them a large sheet of paper and a pen or pencil. Divide the sheet into four columns, with these headings:

- What the adults want
- What the young people want
- What helps
- What hinders.

Make a list of all the things you want and all the changes each of you would like to see. These may range from 'More pocket money' or 'I want to be able to stay out late with my friends' to 'No arguments during meals' or 'No wearing make-up'.

When you look at the list, you may find some of your and the young peoples 'wants' are quite unrealistic or actually seem to work against each other. For instance, if you had said 'I'd like you to tidy your room when asked', and they'd requested, 'We want to keep our own rooms the way we like', you may not feel both of you can be satisfied. Discuss how conflicting wishes help or hinder each other and fill in the next two columns. Discuss what you all want, and why, and talk over how and why the items you've put in the other columns operate.

The next stage is to use this knowledge and understanding to find a realistic solution. Choose one item you all feel is important. Looking at all four columns, decide what it is, what helps and what hinders. Discuss what you can all do to decrease the hindrance and increase the help. Then, do it! Once you have found a way with one item, work your way through the others.

acceptable, good people who deserve your love. It means recognising that we can all behave foolishly, selfishly, badly at times, but that does not mean we are foolish, selfish or bad.

In parenting, as in all life, we tend to underestimate the importance of happiness, laughter and joy. We tend to focus on conflict when we talk about parenting. We worry about whether we are fighting, how and who wins. This means that we often consider the absence of conflict to be the only desirable goal. We concentrate on achieving a quiet life, with no rows, and quiet, obedient teens who are 'no trouble'. What we can forget is that the quiet and obedient child is not necessarily a happy child, and the family without open conflict is not necessarily the family with no problems.

Respect!

It was Doctor Benjamin Spock who, more than fifty years ago, first proposed the totally novel idea at that time that children need cuddling and kissing as much as they needed food. Child care 'experts' before that had said that discipline was more important than love and said that parents should never pick up a crying baby or feed on demand. Spock put in writing what loving, caring parents had instinctively known – you can't spoil a child by openly showing your love.

But the early proscriptive advice still has some effect on us and when children grow into adolescence we may still find ourselves wondering whether cracking down hard may be the right way to do it. Doctor Spock's advice applies to teenagers just as much as it does to children, which is that if you listen to your instinct and listen to your children you are most likely to get it right. Perhaps the most important rule as children get older has to be

'Do as you would be done by'. Think what you would like and need from the people you love and share your life with. Not only do your children probably want this from you, but you are more likely to get it from them if you offer it first. The foundation for everything else is respect. Respecting your child means recognising they have needs, opinions, rights, just as much as you do, and just as much as anyone else. If you want your teenagers to be considerate, thoughtful and helpful to you then you may need to ask yourself whether you are to them. It's not enough to bring them up, to feed them and clothe them and to sacrifice elements of your life to their well-being. If you've never asked them what they would choose, you've never actually thought of how they might feel about this.

Spend time with them

Plenty of parents knock themselves out doing what they see as their best for their children but never actually give the kids what they would most like and value which is themselves. Young people value parents spending time with them and not time doing something but just being with each other. If you've a busy lifestyle, simply allowing your family to have Sunday breakfast in bed with you where you can all read the papers together or watch television can help. Unstructured time can pass on the message that you value them and like being with them. If the only moments you are with them are when you are running them to and from school or other events, at mealtimes or when you have something that needs talking over, or where one of you joins the other watching a programme on television, the impression always is that you are peripheral to each other's lives or only connected when you have to be.

Space to mootch

We tend to feel that there is a value in action and that unless we are getting things done, we're wasting time. A frequent complaint against teenagers, and a common point of argument between teens and parents, is that they are lazy or idle and should be doing something – homework, cleaning their rooms, walking the dog. It's not enough simply to be, we should be doing is the assumption.

The reason kids like 'hanging out' with each other is not because they are lazy or idle. Hanging out makes a particular statement about your feelings for yourself and for the people you are hanging with. If you are relaxed enough to hang out with yourself, you show a level of self-confidence with your own state. When you hang out with friends, you say you value them in themselves, not just for the things you may do together. We tend to have a very Protestant 'work ethic' which demands that we have to be doing something all the time or else feel guilty about wasting time. We pass this on to our teenagers, in effect telling them that we think they are a waste of time unless they are forever doing. It would help parent/child relationships not only to accept that there is nothing wrong in occasionally chilling out but joining them.

One of the reasons we often push teens to be up and doing is their oft-repeated moan of being bored. How many times have you been with young people, who sigh heavily and say 'I'm bored!'? It's hard not to respond by telling them to go and do something, or simply to tell them off. But being bored may often actually mean something else. Sometimes, being bored really means they are depressed. The lethargy and apathy is the moodiness that can be part of the hormonal changes of the teenage years. Or it's an expression of their frustration and powerlessness. What we often need is space. Space to relax and do nothing, without having to feel that we are doing anything wrong.

Paula remembers an adult in her childhood, who obviously knew the value of Doing Nothing:

> ❛I used to be a bit of a terror when I was at school. We would give some teachers hell, especially the student or supply teachers who were only there for a short time. But the teacher I remember most was one we very seldom played up. We all respected her as well as liked her, so we felt particularly good when every so often we'd have a lesson and she'd be in a good mood and just let us have a discussion. Sometimes, you'd ask a question that was a bit off the subject and she'd give a quick answer and pull you back. But every so often, she'd let it run and we'd come out of that period feeling great because we'd had a fun time, but also because we felt that we had got away with it. One year, I went back for a class reunion and somehow this came up in conversation and she laughed. We hadn't got one over her at all. She said there were some times when she knew we were tired – towards the end of term, for instance – and she judged we'd get more done in the long-run if we had a break, especially if we felt we'd earned it ourselves. So on those occasions she'd let us ask a question and allow it to lead into a general talk. ❜

Share your own feelings and concerns

If you want your kids to feel relaxed and happy about sharing their concerns and feelings with you, one way to set the tone is by being open yourself. This doesn't mean burdening your children with worries that would frighten them or be inappropriate for them to know in depth. Young children look to parents to be in control and all-knowing. As they develop, if you keep up a façade of never having problems yourself three barriers may

.ween you and your youngsters. One may be
simply begin to feel totally incompetent. They
these anxieties that no one else seems to share
an. . not enough for them to think, 'Once I become

Exercise: **support systems**

We all need support systems – friends, family and professionals who can be there for both you and your teens. Sometimes, these are people who just share coffee and a chat, or a drink, who can listen to your moans and offer sympathy. Sometimes, they are people who can make suggestions and help you find solutions. And sometimes, they are people who can really bring knowledge, skills or experience to bear on helping us. Write down a list of all the people you can think of that might be there for you.

Think/talk over with your partner or another adult the following:

- What do each of you feel about the people on that list?
- Who would you go to, in which circumstances?
- Why?
- Do you feel secure in your support system or would you like to have more help?
- What can you do to increase support?

We all need support for ourselves in the difficult task of being a parent. Once we could lean over the garden fence or pop next door to an aunt's or sister's, or dash down to the corner shop. By chatting with people who were going through a similar experience and could sympathise, we could all support each other and come to some solution. Now many of our street-corner networking groups have broken down and we need new ones. Many people have found help from parenting groups or by seeking out counselling. Both are actually just another way of finding people who understand, who can help us work out our own solutions to what are very common dilemmas.

an adult, just like my parents, I'll be OK.' Instead, what they think is, 'Nobody else is as stupid as I am and I'm never going to get there.'

The second barrier may evolve because even though they may have an inkling that your invulnerability may be a pose they still may feel that you don't share and therefore can't appreciate exactly how they are feeling. When a teenager shouts, 'You don't understand', they are often speaking from the heart and really feel you can't understand what they are going through.

The third barrier comes about when they know perfectly well that you are struggling with as many anxieties as they are but won't admit it. In that case, kids may be unwilling to open up to you because they see you as insincere, hypocritical and in denial. If you have those problems and can't even face up to them yourself, what help would you be to them if they came to you?

Life stages

Of course, gauging the right way to get on a wavelength with your teenager is all that much harder when they keep jumping back and forth between maturity and childishness. We may accept that all of us can have days when we want to be responsible and in control, and others when we'd like someone else to shoulder the burden and make decisions. What can often be so confusing and irritating to the parents of teenagers is the enormous and apparently inconsistent swings between the way they insist you treat them from one day to the next. Some of their behaviour may also annoy you, but you may not be able to immediately understand why. To overcome this problem, it helps to have some understanding of Life Stages. As each of us grows and develops, there are certain stages we go through, each with certain tasks that have to be fulfilled for us to be able to move on to the next stage in life. These stages aren't fixed – it's perfectly normal and natural for us to reach them at different ages. It's also normal to slip back and forth sometimes, reverting to behaviour usually found at a younger age particularly when we're under stress. The stages, and their main tasks, are outlined here:

Baby: discovers own body and learns to distinguish self from mother. Looks inward, to self and carer.

Child: discovers the outside world and learns the rules of society. Looks to immediate family.

Adolescent: explores sexuality and identity, separates from parents. Looks outward, to friends and outside world.

Young adult: leaves home and establishes lifestyle away from parents. Looks to wider world.

Courtship and marriage: finds other adult and develops loving relationships. Looks to new partner.

Parenthood: adjusts to accept children. Looks inward, to partner and children.

Early midlife: balances own needs with children.

Late midlife: accepts own achievements coming to an end.

Retirement: end of working life.

Old age: accepts end of life round the corner.

You can see how adolescents, going through a stage in life where they should be looking outside and learning how to be themselves, may clash head-on with their parents. Throughout their childhood, you have been focused on the tasks of caring for and protecting them. Just at the time when they want to run out and seize the world, you may be entering that stage in your life when horizons could be shrinking. For women, the menopause is coming. In our society, that still seems to suggest the end of sexual potential. For both men and women, working life may be reaching a climax after which younger people may pass them by. What parents want and need – reassurance, retrenchment, a reaffirming of family bonds – is exactly what young people don't want. Parents may feel a longing to have their importance in their children's eyes confirmed – at the time when young people want to make it clear that their parents are becoming redundant.

Life is all about change

Building self-confidence and self-esteem is one of the vital tasks of the teenage years. We all have a picture of the sort of person we'd like to become. All the experiments of adolescence are an attempt to work through and refine that image. As they develop, they look in the mirror and see the gap between their own self-concept (me as I am) and idealised self (me as I'd like to be). The larger the gap, the more anxious they will be. Teens who have not been allowed the freedom to pursue their own ideas of what they'd like to become are often the ones with the largest gap. And it can be frighteningly easy, and

Hall of Fame

Suggest an area or wall space in the house where anyone can place or stick something they feel is an achievement or they're pleased they or another family member did. We tend to stick up the drawings and paintings of our children when they are young, but this often goes by the board when they get older. Partly it's because they become shy, partly it's because they no longer have the same sort of items to bring home from school for us to display. Even though we might be proud of their achievements, this means they don't get showcased in the same way. A Hall of Fame – in which we should put mementoes of our own points of pride, too – will give you a chance to keep on reminding your young person that you value them. Items can be photos of them, certificates, awards, reports from school or work and notes where you write or they write down what it is you are celebrating.

frighteningly tempting, not to reinforce a good self image, when it will mean they leave us earlier. Every time a young person drops back into 'childish' mode, as a break from the hard work of growing up, we may seize on this as proof that they are still too young to cope on their own. Far from stressing their abilities and triumphs, we may be tempted to emphasise their weaknesses and failures, to keep them by our side.

Teens need to experiment and make their own friends and this shouldn't be felt by you as a rejection. Wanting to throw off your control over them is not the same as wanting to turn their backs on you or your influence. On the contrary, most teens, when they settle into their adult selves, have broadly similar attitudes and beliefs to their parents, even if the style is different. However hard they may be pushing the boundaries, they still need to know they hold firm and are still there. And don't forget, adolescence isn't the only time when you experience enormous and significant changes in your life and yourself. We do tend to think that once you stop 'growing up', you've got there and are now in a 'steady state'. On the contrary, you don't become static because you've become an adult, a parent, a husband or wife. Life is all about change and we are forever learning and altering, adapting and adjusting. Part of the problem is feeling that we should take a stand and stick by what we've got and what we are. Sadly, we often feel that changing ourselves or our minds is somehow an admission of defeat or incompetence. It isn't. Because something becomes inappropriate and wrong doesn't mean it was wrong when we first chose it. But it can be so if we cling to it, way beyond the right time.

An important step to opening the lines of communication with our young people is to accept and acknowledge that they have other influences on and in their lives than you. For children, you are the main source. For teens, it can be friends, school teachers, pop stars and all sorts of

Exercise: **mutual expectations**

Parents often find it difficult to talk with their teenagers when there is a wide gap between what you expected they would be like and what they are like. It can be quite a shock to recognise that the people who share your home, who came from your body and were brought up by you for all this time, have very different ideas of who they are and where they are going. It can be hard enough when talking to them throws up ideas that differ wildly and widely from your own. It can be all the more shocking when their tastes and behaviour underline this in no uncertain terms. You and your teenagers can quickly find yourselves at loggerheads locked in a battle over their clothes, their friends and the music they like. The truth may be that it's not these things individually that are so awful but the fact that they signal so clearly that your children are different from, and separate to, you. Here are some of the ways in which our teens may be different to us:

- Their clothes and hair
- Their musical tastes
- Their leisure interests
- Their body ornamentation
- Their diet (veggie, etc.)
- Their sexual choices – gender and activity
- Their friendship choices
- Their education ambitions
- Their job choice.

Add any others you can think of your own. Sit down with another adult and discuss:

- What exactly is different
- Why you don't like it
- Whether you and your parents had similar arguments
- Why these differences matter to you.

Exercise: **examining beliefs and behaviour**

It's often useful to examine your beliefs and behaviour. What you do says as much to your children as what you say. And you undermine your own precepts when there is a conflict between the two. One flashpoint for teens and parents are the rules we ask them (or tell them) to keep. Sometimes, those rules make sense. Asking them not to drink and drive is an elementary bit of road sense you would prefer to apply to your own behaviour. But are all our rules as useful? Sometimes, rules might have outlived their usefulness and could profitably be amended. Not allowing them to use your sound system might have been reasonable when they were 6, but a 16-year-old could be careful of your equipment if you give him or her your trust.

Sometimes, a rule could be altered from being an inflexible stricture to something to be discussed. Not staying up late on a school night can be negotiated on some occasions. And asking them to keep to a rule you regularly flout yourself – not swearing, not smoking – is asking for rebellion. Telling them these are things that only grown-ups may do only makes them desirable. How many of these do you agree with?

Divide a piece of paper into four columns. Then add some of the rules in your house to the left-hand column, such as:

Don't drink and drive
Don't use intoxicating substances unwisely
Don't be sarcastic
Don't swear
Don't be rude
Keep your room tidy

Write the following headings at the top of the other three columns and tick as appropriate.

I always keep these myself ☐	I sometimes keep these myself ☐	I never keep these myself ☐

Sit down with your family and talk over the following:

- Where did these rules come from?
- Why do you think they are important?
- Which ones might be altered?

other people, real and imaginary, in actual contact or in touch through various media. Being supportive and trusting them is the best way to keep some influence, just as letting them go is the best way to make them want to come home. Above all, research suggests that peer pressure is more likely to be harmful and lead them into trouble if you have failed them, by not being available or by being critical and judgmental, than if you are flexible and accepting. Making friends welcome and giving them space, and not assuming the worst, can mean they don't have to court trouble just to defy you.

Risk taking

The truth is that there is very little that your young people can do that is irrevocable. What's the worst that can happen? They break the law? Yes, but many of us do, as young people, and the vast majority grow out of it and become upright citizens. Use drugs? Yes, but define your terms. Most of the present generation of parents have used a substance illegally at some point (cannabis, pills, acid) and no longer do. Even more still use substances that are as dangerous and/or addictive (nicotine, alcohol) but are legal. Any habit can be broken. Get pregnant? Not quite as disastrous as you might think. This is not to be casual or dismissive about the dangers out there. They are real and sometimes can lead to tragedy or can divert a teenage life down a path we might not have wanted or expected. But our fears aren't always realistic and we can over react. If we can hang in there, being supportive and accepting, they can grow out of crime, drug use, anything.

Young people take risks as a way of testing boundaries. Not just the boundaries of what you say they can and cannot do, but also the boundaries of what they are and are not capable of. It's important to them and their future competence as adults that they make these experiments and try new things out. In wanting to keep them safe, you may find yourself on a one-way track to conflict. And if you succeed in discouraging them, the results may not be what you expect or even want. When young people are prevented from finding out for themselves, they may grow up unsure of their own abilities and lacking in the confidence to make their own discoveries. You'll have taught them not to trust themselves, that they can't be expected to become able to handle certain things, and this lesson may bite deep. Young people who don't go through a period of experiment and change as teenagers, may then try to catch up later on, when it's no longer appropriate. The young adult who acts recklessly and foolishly may be the one who never learnt how to do so as a teenager.

Win-win

Your aim should be to turn every encounter within your family into a win-win scenario. There are four possible scenarios in any face-to-face:

- Lose-lose: both of you come away from the encounter feeling bruised, battered and that you have lost
- Win-lose: one of you comes away knowing you feel triumphant and that you have won, the other person feels unhappy and that they have lost
- Lose-win: one of you comes away knowing you feel unhappy and that you have lost, the other person feels triumphant and that they have won
- Win-win: both of you come away knowing both of you feel good and that the encounter was equally satisfying and successful for you both.

Win-lose scenarios may be the preferred prescription for a sporting engagement, when you might not feel any-

Exercise: **strokes**

We all need to be rewarded, to be praised and thanked and appreciated. Sometimes we forget how much we need to value others, and to be valued by them. Often, we forget how easy it is to give pleasure and how a little would mean a lot. Counsellors call the sort of action that gives a lift to morale 'a stroke'. Strokes can be spoken – telling someone you love them, thanking them for helping you or saying you value them. Or they can be shown by contact – hugging or kissing someone or giving them a back rub. Or they can be acted out – making them a cup of coffee, giving them a small present or doing a chore you know they'd like done. Make a list of strokes you'd like to give and one of strokes you'd like to receive and ask the rest of your family to do the same. Discuss them and agree to give each other at least one stroke each today.

thing was achieved unless one of you – preferably you – did better than the other person. But it's a losing formula when you apply it to personal relationships. Every time one of you walks away feeling diminished, the relationship itself has lost out.

Not what but how

Making any change in our lives is nerve wracking. But it isn't change itself that is difficult or causes problems but how we manage it. It's our apprehensions and anxieties that stop us, make the transition difficult and ultimately spoil our chances of making a difference. We often talk about young people 'Having an attitude' and we mean having a bad, aggressive or unhelpful attitude. But we all 'have attitude' – and the worst sort to have is the negative, hopeless, 'I can never make a difference', type. Parents need to get attitude – the attitude that says ,'I'm OK, my kids are OK and we can make a difference!' Try it!

Chapter 4
How to talk

It's not always easy to change your style of speech and approach and it may be tempting to feel that you've got this far without total disaster so why invite the discomfort and embarrassment of altering. Yes, it may be hard work, yes it may initially seem to cause more problems than it solves but the fact of the matter is that communicative parenting really does work. It's also never too late to start because in a lot of ways it's retroactive. When you go through the process of looking at your own background and feelings and how that has affected you in the here and now with your own offspring, you can actually go back and rectify a lot of the misunderstandings of the past. Even if they are late teenagers and about to leave home, by explaining why you might have done what you did, argument and resentment can be put to rest. It only needs the first step, which is for you to take responsibility for your own feelings and for action.

First, as we have already discussed, we need to explore our own pasts and understand ourselves. Take the time to heal your own childhood disappointments and boost your own self-esteem and confidence in order to 'break the chain'. Part of this process may be examining your own motives for being a parent. After all, your children didn't ask to be here, so what are you getting or hoping to get out of being a parent? Why you had them – your expectations and fantasies – may have a lot to do with what happens between you. Once you have an insight into what underlies your relationship you'll be able to see what you expected and needed from them. You may then be able to identify key behaviour patterns that pass on important messages, and can choose to strengthen or to modify them.

As teenagers grow and evolve, both physically and emotionally, so too do your rules and responses. What you want from them and what they need from you has to change as they age. The demands that you make upon, and the leeway you allow a 13-year-old will necessarily be very different to what you would expect of an 18-year-old. 'Good enough' parents have to be jugglers, sometimes keeping half-a-dozen balls in the air. Not only do you have to accept that you do have to change as your children grow older, but you may have to perform the difficult balancing act between different children of different ages. You are far more likely to get this right and to have it work if you are enlisting those young people in a consensus. If they can see an evolution, and feel consulted and involved, they are far more likely to co-operate. The skills of communication are essentially the same, whether the child is 2 or 20, and it's never too late or too early to start.

> ### You don't need to always have the answers

What young people need above all is not a walking encyclopaedia but someone who will be responsive to them. One educationalist, Sol Gordon, called it being an askable parent. That is, someone your kids want to talk to, someone they feel listens, is always approachable and honest and won't make judgements. To be askable, we need to be able to be flexible. There are rules, situations, arguments, battles that are important, and there are some that are not. Know the difference! It's often only by giving way on one that we can negotiate being able to insist on another. What is important is consistency of attitude, not of reaction. Saying yes to a late night at a disco with friends doesn't mean you've given up on sensible bedtimes for ever. It means you and your teen have talked and come to an agreement for this occasion.

Being consistent also doesn't always mean both saying the same thing. You as parents can disagree over certain aspects or occasions. Consistent parenting is when you and your partner may have different ideas of what is required but do agree on the essentials – safety, feeling and showing mutual respect, recognising everyone's rights, and keeping in touch.

Open and shut

One stand-up comedian has the lovely idea that MI5 and the CIA should recruit teenagers as spies. Well, as he says, the enemy could get nothing out of them if they were captured and interrogated. 'Where were you going?' 'Out.' 'Who were you seeing?' 'Nobody you'd know.' 'What were you doing?' 'Nothing.' There is a serious side to this, which is that the questions we so often throw at our young people dictate the way they answer. There are two types of ways of eliciting information from people. The first is the closed question. This is when you ask a question that can, and sometimes can only, be answered with a yes, a no or a short statement. 'Where were you going?' and 'Who were you seeing?' are good examples. So is 'Did you have a good time at school today?' or 'What did you do in school?'. They both simply beg to be dismissed with 'Not a lot!' Think of some of the closed questions you might ask your young people.

There are two problems with closed questions. One is that they can stop the conversation dead. The person being asked the question can just respond to the immediate query by saying yes, no or not a lot, and need go no further. Try it with your partner or another adult. You'll find it takes quite some effort to elaborate further than just answering the immediate query.

- Did you have a good day?
- What's for dinner?
- Was the bus on time this morning?

- What do you do for a living?
- Are you going away for your holidays?
- Did you have a good weekend?

Even more important, such questions tend to push the person being asked into only giving you a short answer. The reason for this is that a closed question suggests or even tells the person what you want to hear. 'Did you have a good time at school today?' implies that you expect them to have enjoyed school and goes some way towards saying that if they answer 'No', you might come down heavily on them to explain what they're doing wrong.

An opener carries with it a different message. Some examples of openers would be:

- Tell me about your day.
- You seem fed up/in good spirits.
- I'm starving and I'm looking forward to dinner tonight.
- You look as if you had a good/tiring/disappointing time last night.
- I've been thinking about that concert you said you wanted to go to. Tell me some more about it.

Exercise: **turning closed questions into openers**

Example:

Closed **What sort of a time do you think this is?**

Open   **It's later than you agreed to get home. I was really worried about what might have kept you.**

Closed **You're not going out dressed like that, are you?**
Open

Closed **Call that a room, it's a pigsty?**
Open

Closed **Why don't you ever do the washing-up?**
Open

Closed **Is that the way you talk to your parents?**
Open

An example of what happens when you use closed questions with a teenager would be this dialogue between Sandy and her daughter Gita. Sandy has come home from the supermarket to find her daughter Gita watching television.

	What they said	What they felt	What they thought	How it came over
Sandy	*Did you have a good day at school today, Gita?*	Tired, fed up.	I've been knocking myself out for this family and what thanks do I get?	She's asking just to establish she's home.
Gita	*(grunts)*	Sorry for herself.	I've been told off and put down in front of the whole class for something I didn't do, had an argument with my best friend and I think the boy I fancy has asked someone else out.	Self-absorbed.
Sandy	*Do you want a cup of tea?*	Exasperated.	Oh, God, here we go again but I'll make an effort.	I just want your attention.
Gita	*(grunts)*	Got at.	She just wants me to come and help – she never cares how I feel.	Rude.

	What they said	**What they felt**	**What they thought**	**How it came over**
Sandy	*Don't just sit there, come and give me a hand.*	Annoyed.	Why do teenagers always just slump around? They haven't a care in the world, they're just lazy!	So who cares if you've got worries?
Gita	*(grunts)*	Miserable.	Why doesn't she ever ask me how I feel?	Petulant.
Sandy	*Come on, Gita, don't just sit there.*	Angry.	For heaven's sakes, why does she always sulk so?	Imperious.
Gita	*(grunts)*	On the verge of tears.	What's the use of anything?	Miserable.
Sandy	*Anything wrong? Come on, talk to me! What's the matter?*	Alerted.	Perhaps there is something wrong.	Prying.
Gita	*Why do you always assume I've got problems?!*	Needy.	I want to be hugged and be a baby again!	In a temper.
Sandy	*Well, excuse me for caring!*	Affronted and rejected.	When I do try, this is what I get.	Dismissive and angry.
Gita	*Oh, leave me alone!*	Discounted.	Nobody cares!	In a tantrum.

Now look at what happens when Sandy uses some communication skills to find out what is really happening, and doesn't assume the worst about Gita's behaviour. Even the way that Gita comes over will change because of the way that Sandy is looking at her.

	What they said	**What they felt**	**What they thought**	**How it came over**
Sandy	*What sort of a day did you have, Gita?*	Tired, fed up.	I need to get all this put away, have a cuppa, make a meal.	Busy but receptive.
Gita	*(grunts)*	Sorry for herself.	I've been told off and put down in front of the whole class for something I didn't do, had an argument with my best friend and I think the boy I fancy has asked someone else out.	Troubles of my own.
Sandy	*You don't sound too happy.*	Alerted.	My child needs me – something's up.	Open.
Gita	*(grunts)*	In need of a listening ear.	I wish I could explain.	Sad.
Sandy	*Can I come and sit with you?*	Concerned.	I'll just be with her and see if she wants to talk – the shopping and cooking can wait.	Ready to listen.

	What they said	What they felt	What they thought	How it came over
Gita	*(grunts)*	Comforted.	Where do I begin?	There's loads on my mind.
Sandy	*(sits quietly)*	Sympathetic.	Is it school, friends? Something is bothering her.	There for her daughter.
Gita	*I had an awful day.*	Relief.	She'll understand.	Needing a shoulder to cry on.
Sandy	*You had a bad day?*	Concerned.	She sounds miserable, I wonder what happened.	Sympathetic.
Gita	*Yeah. Mr Jones told me off in front of the whole class.*	Upset.	I know she'll hear me out.	Affronted.
Sandy	*He told you off in front of everyone? I should think that hurt your feelings.*	Upset on her behalf.	Let's hear the whole story.	Non-judgmental.
Gita	*Yes, he said I'd given in my homework late but it wasn't fair because I'd put it in his pigeonhole, it's not my fault he didn't pick it up till this morning.*	Embarrassed.	Well, maybe I was a bit late but he still shouldn't have shown me up.	Facing up to it.

	What they said	What they felt	What they thought	How it came over
Sandy	*You sound fed up about that.*	Accepting.	I can see why she felt upset.	Listening.
Gita	*That's not all. I had an argument with Beth.*	Feeling better.	But what I'm really upset about is this.	Relaxing.
Sandy	*You had a fight with your best friend?*	Sympathetic.	Is there more?	Receptive.
Gita	*And there's a boy I fancy and I think he's asked someone else out.*	Tearful.	She won't laugh at me.	Telling the final secret.
Sandy	*So you're feeling pretty miserable.*	Empathetic.	Oh, I know how that feels!	Loving.
Gita	*Yeah. But you know what, I'm going to call Beth. Perhaps she's over it. Thanks Mum, you're the best.*	Listened to and hopeful.	Maybe I did take this too seriously.	Looking forward.
Sandy	*Glad to be of service!*	Relieved.	Taking the time to listen does make a difference!	Accepting and trusting.

Learning to listen

To truly communicate with someone else, and especially
young people, you first have to listen. This may sound
obvious, but how many times have you had a so-called
conversation with another person and realised from the
beginning that they weren't listening to a word you said?
How often do you talk to someone, and know that
they're simply waiting for a gap in your words to jump in
with their pre-prepared speech? And how often have you
talked with someone and simply not known whether
they were listening or interested, because their attention
appeared to be elsewhere? It's more than a little off-
putting to be opening your heart and have your confi-
dant's eyes fixed on the distance. The ability to listen
sensitively is a skill we have to learn, not an art we're
born with. Nobody can read minds – not even parents of
their offspring, however much we'd like to think we
know what is going on in their skulls. If you want to
understand what they think and feel, why they do certain things and how to get on the same wavelength, you
have to enlist their point of view. And if you want to
make it clear that you are attending, you need to know
how.

It's actually very easy – depressingly easy – to stop
someone from opening up to you. As parents, we want to
be available and sympathetic, but how often do we interrupt, impose our own ideas, finish sentences, switch off,
talk too much or contradict the other person when we're
trying to communicate? We may feel, while doing all
these things, that we're involved with the dialogue and
these interventions show how much we may be engaging
with them. From the other point of view, they may be
doing nothing of the sort. Have a look at these dialogues
between Bernie and his daughter Naomi, who has just
arrived home from school.

Bernie Had a good day, dear?

Naomi Well, not really Dad. Mrs Brown got on my case and . . .

Bernie Oh, teachers, I had some terrible ones when I was at school.

Naomi No, she's usually OK but today . . .

Bernie Sometimes the ones you like are the worst because you expect too much of them.

Naomi Yes but the point is . . . .

Bernie You've just got to hang in there and be firm.

Naomi Yeah, but Dad, I had this . . .

Bernie Don't let it get to you, that's what I say.

Naomi Oh, forget it!

Bernie Hey, was there something you wanted to say to me?

Loving, caring, keen to sympathise – but constantly interrupting. Is it any wonder Naomi gave up?

Bernie Had a good day, dear?

Naomi Well, not really Dad. Mrs Brown got on my case and told me off for not doing the science project the way she'd said we should.

Bernie Well, I wouldn't stand for that. If you had a good idea you should stick with it and tell her where to get off!

Naomi Yeah, but Dad, she sort of had a point . . .

Bernie You should talk to the Head of Department and see what other people think about this. I mean, showing a bit of initiative, that's admirable.

Naomi Yeah, well thanks Dad (mutters; for nothing!).

Bernie was trying to help, but by imposing his own ideas on what he thought his daughter should do, gave her no real support or understanding of the situation and her feelings about it.

Bernie Had a good day, dear?

Naomi Well, not really Dad. Mrs Brown got on my case and told me off for not doing the science project . . .

Bernie . . . in time?

Naomi No, the way she'd said we should. The thing is Dad, she said we had to . . .

Bernie . . . do it the way it was in your books, is that the problem?

Naomi No, we had to do it in groups. The problem was . . .

Bernie Oh, you wanted to do it on your own and she made you pair up.

Naomi No, I wanted to do it with Debbie . . .

Bernie Oh, she split you up from your friends. Well, I'm sure she had a good reason for doing that love.

Naomi Yeah (sighs) thanks Dad (mutters; for nothing!).

In this case, her father's constant interruptions meant he couldn't hear what she was trying to tell him.

Bernie Had a good day, dear?

Naomi Well, not really Dad. Mrs Brown got on my case and told me off for not doing the science project the way she'd said we should. Dad, you listening?

Bernie Hmmm? Yes, of course sweetie. Mrs Brown gave you a bad mark.

Naomi No, she told me off.

Bernie Uh-huh

Naomi It's not fair, she never listens to me. Dad?

Bernie Well, I'm sure she had a reason. Have you seen my car keys? I'm sure I put them down somewhere around here.

Naomi Oh, Dad!

Bernie What? Look, I'm in a hurry, what was it you wanted?

Naomi Never mind.

Bernie might have been there in body but he was hardly available to his daughter.

Bernie Had a good day, dear?

Naomi Well, not really Dad. Mrs Brown got on my case and told me off for not doing the science project the way she'd said we should.

Bernie Oh, well, that's nothing. You should have seen me when I was your age, I was always in trouble. You couldn't find a day when I wasn't in the principal's office, hauled up for some misdemeanour or other. Never did me any harm, though.

Naomi Yeah, but Dad, it wasn't fair.

Bernie It never is, is it? I mean, teachers have their own way of doing things and you just have to put up with it. I remember one teacher we had and she was a terror! She used to creep up behind you in class and catch you doodling or reading stuff you shouldn't be reading.

Naomi Dad, I was just trying to do this project.

Bernie We never had projects in my day, it was all class work and exams. You don't know when you're well off, believe me.

Naomi Yes Dad.

Here, Bernie probably felt he was being a fabulous Dad – supportive, understanding and on his daughter's side. He was so keen to show her he understood because he'd 'been there', he hardly listened to a word she was saying.

Bernie Had a good day, dear?

Naomi Well, not really Dad. Mrs Brown got on my case and told me off for not doing the science project the way she'd said we should.

Bernie I'm sure she didn't do that, dear.

Naomi Yes she did. She said I should have done it the way she said, but . . .

Bernie I'm sure you misunderstood her Naomi.

Naomi But Dad, it wasn't fair!

Bernie Oh, I'm sure it was sweetie. You have to learn to put up with these things.

In all these scenarios, the way Bernie responded put up barriers to Naomi confiding in him or getting what she wanted and needed from the conversation. Each time, however much he might have wanted to be sympathetic and helpful, by interrupting, imposing his ideas, finishing sentences, switching off, talking too much or contradicting, he stopped Naomi dead in her tracks. Think about the people you might know or have seen on television who you would say are 'good listeners'. What is it that they do to make you feel comfortable and able to confide in them, and get what you need from the exchange? There is a skill to listening in a way that opens people up instead of shutting them up: the skill of active listening. Try the listening exercise below, with another person – an adult or a teenager.

Active listening

The problem with chipping in with your own ideas is that it often doesn't help as much as stop your teenager come to an understanding and a solution. Often, your questions aren't really there to help the other person but to show that you know better. And simply saying 'I under-

---

Exercise: **active listening**

The rules are that each of you should take a turn being the listener and the speaker. Use a kitchen timer or alarm clock to time an initial two-minute period. The speaker gets two minutes to talk, on any subject they choose. Their only task is to keep talking. The listener's task is to hear and encourage the other person to talk – but without saying a single word. No interruptions, no questions, no comments. What they should do is help the speaker along with nods and the sort of 'Uh-huh', 'Um' and 'Ah?' sounds that say, 'Yes, go on, I'm hearing you.'

You may like to try this a few times. After the first attempt, talk over with your companion how it felt. How did it feel just to listen and not ask questions? How did it feel to be listened to, knowing you wouldn't be interrupted in any way?

---

stand' frequently begs for the retort 'No you don't!' But making it clear you are listening and taking in what the other person is saying can be reassuring and empowering. Being heard gives the speaker a chance to hear themselves, too. Instead of wasting energy on making you pay attention, bring the subject back to what they wanted to discuss or argue with advice that is inappropriate, they can bounce their own ideas off you and see their own way to a resolution. It often feels very awkward and odd at first, on both sides. You'll get used to it, and be amazed at exactly how effective it is as a tool. Once you've tried active listening, go one stage further and add reflective listening to your skills.

Reflective listening

Having your own words coming back at you not only gives the speaker the chance to hear what they've said and clarify it, but it makes them fully reassured that they have been understood. It often feels very awkward and odd at first, on both sides. But by using the exercise overleaf, you will get used to it, and be amazed at exactly how effective it is as a tool.

You can see how Bernie got on with Naomi when he tried using both active and reflective listening skills.

Bernie Had a good day, dear?

Naomi Well, not really Dad. Mrs Brown got on my case and told me off for not doing the science project the way she'd said we should.

Bernie Uh-huh?

Naomi Yes. She said we had to do it in groups and I wanted to do it with Debbie and Beth.

Bernie Ummm?

Naomi Well, Debbie was away all last week and Beth and me, we thought she was coming back, so we did it together, 'cos we thought she'd be back in time to catch up.

Exercise: **reflective listening**

The rules are that each of you should take a turn being the listener and the speaker. Use a kitchen timer or alarm clock to time an initial two-minute period. The speaker gets two minutes to talk, on any subject they choose. Their only task is to keep talking. The listener's task is to mirror back to the speaker what they say to you. So, this time, instead of saying 'Uh-huh' or 'Um' to what they say, repeat it. You can use their words or your own words. Reflective listening isn't just parroting, it's rephrasing and checking, which means you don't have to get it entirely right first time, every time – the speaker will correct you and it still works. The point is that you are making the attempt to listen and hear what they are saying, not putting your words into their mouth. It will sound a lot stranger to the person doing the reflective listening than to the speaker. Useful phrases to use in front of your mirrored speech may be 'It sounds as if you're saying . . .', 'I imagine you're feeling . . .', 'It seems to me that what you're saying is . . .', 'What I hear you saying is . . .'.

You may like to try this a few times. After the first attempt, talk over with your companion how it felt. How did it feel to be focusing on the other person's words in order to be able to repeat them back accurately? How did it feel to have the other person repeating your words back at you?

Bernie You thought Debbie would be back in time for the three of you to finish the project together.

Naomi Yes, but she's got 'flu so she isn't even going to be back this week. But Mrs Brown just ripped us off for doing it in a pair, she said it needed at least three of us and why hadn't we joined up with someone else? That wasn't fair, was it?

Bernie I can see you feel upset about this.

Naomi Well, I suppose we should have told her last week that we were waiting for Debbie.

Bernie Uh-huh.

Naomi It was a bit silly not to let her know, wasn't it?

Bernie You think it was silly not to let her know.

Naomi Well, maybe the best thing would be to talk to her tomorrow and explain and say we're sorry for not having told her sooner.

Bernie So you're going to talk with Mrs Brown tomorrow.

Naomi Yup. Thanks for helping, Dad.

In this last example, Naomi's Dad used another helpful technique, which is giving feelings a name. When Naomi said 'That wasn't fair, was it?' he thought about what her emotions might be, and put a name to them by responding 'I can see you feel upset about this.' If he'd been wrong, and she was angry or fed up or embarrassed, by that stage in the conversation the chances are that she would have corrected him without breaking the flow, and gone on. When you have the tone right in an exchange, you can check out what might be being said without it meaning that you seem to be misunderstanding.

Giving feelings a name

Giving feelings a name is an important part of valuing and validating what your young people feel, and what they are. Arguments or lack of understanding come about between young people and their parents so often because we don't accept what they are saying.

Teenager I hate you!

Parent You don't mean that.

Teenager I've had an awful day!

Parent I'm sure it's not as bad as all that, dear.

Teenager That guy at the swimming pool was mean to me!

Parent Don't be silly, he was just doing his job.

Teenager I'm hungry!
Parent You can't be, we've just eaten.

Teenager I'm fed up. I wish I was dead!
Parent You're exaggerating.

Teenager It's not fair!
Parent You're just tired.

Teenager Nobody ever listens to me!
Parent Calm down – stop shouting.

Teenager Nothing ever goes right for me!
Parent Don't be so intense – you take things so seriously.

Because what they are saying is something we don't want to hear, we deny it. When you deny a feeling it doesn't go away, but the person expressing that emotion is left with a triple load. They still have the uncomfortable emotion, because even though they've tried to offload on to you and thus deal with it, you've shoved it back into their arms. They also have the additional emotional burden of anger, hurt or bafflement (or all three) with you for not hearing. Worse of all, they must grapple with confusion and distrust of their own feelings. They've clearly announced their emotional state to us, and we've said it doesn't exist. Have that happen enough times in your life and you do start to doubt your own responses.

Of course, the reason we, as parents, do this is not necessarily because we don't believe our young people are going through these difficulties. We genuinely believe that if we can argue away the feelings, deny their very existence, we can banish them. Alas, it doesn't work like that. But another aspect is that we see their response as a comment on and criticism of ourselves. If our children feel bad, we assume we are failing them and we rush to make it better in the way we have been taught – by arguing over the existence of the bad feeling. We feel uncomfortable in admitting to the existence of negative emotions as if allowing that they exist will show us up and be bad parenting. It's mostly about our own anger, anxiety, lack of self-confidence and self-esteem, because we do feel this is the only way we can help, as if accepting the unhappiness will intensify the distress and denying them will make it vanish into thin air.

By giving feelings a name, you soon find that allowing to bad feelings is the first step in learning to handle them and to letting go of them.

Acknowledging emotions

Good listening is about allowing the other person an opinion, not surrendering your own. You can listen to what they say, and accept that this is how they might be feeling or seeing a situation, without having to agree with their point of view or condoning what they think. In fact, sometimes being a 'Yes Person' and agreeing with everything they say prevents them from progressing. Side with them as they protest the teacher has been unfair or their best friend was horrible, and you prevent your teen from working through their emotions to accept that they might have contributed to the difficulty and need to compromise themselves. But by acknowledging their emotions and accepting that they exist, you tell them they are acceptable and valued by you. Everyone is entitled to be angry sometimes, and entitled to have conflicting feelings, too.

Teenager I hate you!
Parent I can hear you feel that you hate me at the moment.

Teenager I've had an awful day!
Parent You feel you've had a bad time today.

Teenager That guy at the swimming pool was mean to me!

Parent You feel he was mean to you.

Teenager I'm hungry!

Parent You still feel hungry, even though we've just eaten.

Teenager I'm fed up. I wish I was dead!

Parent You're really feeling bad.

Teenager It's not fair!

Parent You're feeling very hard done-by.

Teenager Nobody ever listens to me!

Parent I can hear you're feeling unappreciated.

Teenager Nothing ever goes right for me!

Parent You are feeling as if things aren't going right for you.

We spend a great deal of time and effort denying angry and negative feelings and trying to pretend to ourselves and everyone else that we don't feel like that. How many times have you said 'I'm fine, nothing's wrong!' when you might really have liked to scream 'I feel TERRIBLE!' and been given a hug? Teenagers have strong and genuine emotions. They feel, and it's only our teaching that makes them lose that facility to be in touch with their emotions. We call this process of distancing ourselves from feelings 'being civilised'. You don't allow them to have negative feelings because you won't allow yourself to have them and you feel they will overwhelm you and get out of control. But reflecting and allowing feelings doesn't prolong them or enlarge them or make them real where otherwise they would not emerge. What it does is allow them to be discharged. Even temper tantrums are actually very healthy – a good shout, moan or sob gets it all out of the system.

Are you fine?

The next time someone asks you how you feel and you say
'Fine', reflect on this alternative definition for that word.
It can mean 'OK'. It can also mean

F ucked up
I nsecure
N eurotic and
E motionally unstable.

Which usually describes it just about perfectly, doesn't it?

Accepting their feelings

Accept a young person's feelings and you will find
several advantages flow from this. For example, you may
discover more about the situation than you originally
realised.

Teenager That guy at the swimming pool was mean to
me!

Parent You feel he was mean to you.

Teenager Yeah, he confiscated our towels when we left
them at the side of the pool and we had to each pay
him a quid to get them back.

Parent You had to pay him money to get your towels
back?

Teenager There are no notices about not leaving your
towels on the side but he says it's untidy. I think he's
running a scam, don't you?

Parent It certainly sounds odd. What do you want to do
about it?

Teenager Would you come with us next week, and we
can speak to the manager? I can get Sam to come too
and you can back us up.

Parent That sounds like a good idea.

Part of the wish to deny feelings is the fear that we can't do anything to help them, and the helplessness that this engenders. You may be surprised to find that, sometimes, just acknowledging an emotion diminishes it.

Teenager I've had an awful day!
Parent You feel you've had a bad time today.
Teenager I got caught in the rain and missed my bus and then I found I'd left my bus pass at home and I had to pay full fare.
Parent You feel pretty fed up.
Teenager Yeah, well. Thanks Mum! What's for supper?

Listening doesn't mean giving in

Listening to kids doesn't mean giving in to them. By accepting what they feel, you can also then go on to say you can't do anything about it unless they tell you what they're angry about. Sometimes, listening to and accepting the emotion also leads to your accepting a compromise on what you all do.

Teenager I hate you!
Parent I can hear you feel that you hate me at the moment.
Teenager You're horrible!
Parent You're really angry with me, aren't you?
Teenager Yes, I am.
Parent Can you tell me what you're angry about?
Teenager You never asked me what I felt about going to see grandma this weekend. It's Paul's birthday and he's having a party and I'll have to miss it.
Parent Yes, I'm sorry, I should have talked to you and everyone. The reason we're going this weekend is that this is the only time your father and I and Gran were all free. Would you like to give her a ring and see if you could go down and see her another weekend on your own? If there was, you could stay with Paul for the weekend. Or you could join us on Sunday.

Accepting and then negotiating also means you may find they accept the limits you would like to put in place. You can listen and accept what they are saying, and agree that this is what they feel, without having to agree that you are going to do what they want. You allow the feelings but not necessarily the action, and you may open the door to a compromise.

Parent I can hear that you'd really like to go to this all-night party with your friends. It sounds as if this is important to you. I'm still going to have to say no to letting you stay out all night.

Teenager OK Dad, I suppose that is a bit much. Could we stay until 1am?

Parent If I can come and pick you up, yes.

Teenager Cool!

Give it in fantasy

Sometimes, simply being able to recognise how strongly your teenagers want this particular thing can help. You may even want to grant their wishes, but in fantasy not reality, to let them know how much you see their point of view and would like to agree.

Teenager I'm fed up. I wish I was dead!

Parent You're really feeling bad.

Teenager Life is awful!

Parent You sound as if things are pretty hopeless.

Teenager Oh, Mum, I'm never going to get a boyfriend I like.

Parent I wish I could wave a magic wand and make the perfect man appear for you.

Teenager That's silly!

Parent Maybe, but I wish I could, because I would if I could.

Teenager I know you would. Thanks Mum.

Giving feelings a name and active, reflective listening are also part of valuing and enjoying your children. Being enthusiastic about them and what they do and praising them is far more effective than criticising or directing them. Constantly teaching your teens by saying, 'Do this. Do it this way', is actually as forbidding and disempowering as constantly telling 'No' and 'Don't'. It's certainly less effective than encouraging them to learn how to do it their own way. Telling them what not to do deprives them of self-esteem and self-confidence. Telling them what to do deprives them of trust. You don't trust them to work it out themselves and you stop them learning how.

Bulletin Board

Give your kids a boost and show them how much you value them, their interests and their ideas by having a House Bulletin Board. Suggest an area or wall space in the house where anyone can place or stick up something they'd like to bring to everyone else's attention – a cartoon, a newspaper article, a picture. It could be something that amused them or they thought was interesting, alarming or relevant. Anything, in other words, that caught their attention and would like to share.

'I' messages

Many of the circular arguments in which we find ourselves stuck are due to the 'You' messages we tend to use. Think back to the last argument you had, and what did you say to your teenager? Was it something along these lines?

- 'You're so lazy.'
- 'Why don't you pull yourself together?'
- 'You never listen to a thing I say!'
- 'You always argue with me.'

Each statement has one thing in common, which is that they are 'You' messages. Each is a label and an accusation. You're telling them that whatever you're objecting about is their fault. Each demands they should change to do something the way you want. Most of all, each statement says you don't like them for being like that. None of these statements gives a proper account of why you are objecting. They don't suggest a constructive solution. They don't allow for discussion. And, worst of all, they often say you know they can't change because that's the way they are. 'You are' invariably becomes 'I am' as the young person concerned takes in the criticism and accepts it as a true description of the way they are. 'You' messages seldom make the person being accused sit up, smile sweetly and say, 'Hey, I see what you mean! You're right, I'll do it different!' They usually make the subject feel angry, defensive, useless, humiliated and/or hurt. And, of course, lumbered for all time with that label.

The opposite of a 'You' message is an 'I' message. 'I' messages are about what the speaker feels and thinks, not what they think about the other person. Instead of saying 'You're so lazy', an 'I' message might be, 'I feel upset when I come home and find your chores haven't been done. It means I have to do extra work and I resent that.' Instead of blaming or being judgmental, an 'I' message puts across your feelings and says how and why you feel the other person's actions have contributed to this. But you are not saying that they meant to do it this way. You are asking them to think about how you feel, but you also invite them to talk about it. They might have had an understandable reason for not doing what you had wanted, which a snap response from you might prevent them from explaining. When people use strong 'I' messages they can be pleasantly surprised by having the other person say, 'Oh, I really didn't know you felt like this. Can we come to an agreement?'

The key phrase for using 'I' messages is 'I feel . . .'. But to use it so it makes sense, and really works, you do have to be genuine. It's no good just slapping 'I feel' on the beginning of a question, statement or complaint; 'I feel you're being a pain-in-the-butt' is a 'You' message in very poor disguise! To use them effectively, you really do need to confront your own emotions and come clean about how you are reacting and what you are feeling about the situation.

Exercise: **turning 'you' messages into 'I' messages**

Look at these 'you' messages. Can you turn them into 'I' messages? Add some of your own.

Example:

'You' message **You've got a memory like a sieve – I told you to feed the cat and you've forgotten again.**

'I' message **Tibbles gets hungry and I feel annoyed when I ask you to do something and it doesn't get done.**

'You' message **You never listen to a thing I say!**
'I' message

'You' message **You look terrible, why do you have to wear your hair like that?**
'I' message

'You' message **You're so untidy – why do you always leave your room in such a mess?**
'I' message

'You' message **You're so inconsiderate – you took my best jacket out of the wardrobe and just left it in a heap.**
'I' message

❛I'll never forget the time Alan turned up at his older brother's wedding with his hair in a brutal crew-cut. I was furious with him and nearly told Mick to get one of his friends to be best man instead. Alan has always been a bit of a rebel so it never occurred to be that this was anything other than a silly joke on his part. I gave him a right telling off and told him he was going to ruin the wedding photographs. I was just so mad at him, I said he was thoughtless and selfish and for once in his life he should have given a moment's consideration to other people, and he just stood there and took it silently. It was Mick who told me weeks later that Alan hadn't had his hair cut like that deliberately. What had happened was that some of his sillier friends had got him in a rugby tackle at the stag party the week before and shaved one side of his head. On balance, he decided an all-over cut was the best thing to do. I felt so awful that he hadn't been able to tell me that was the reason – but then, I never gave him a chance to tell me, did I? ❜

Of course, 'I' messages only work if you really are expressing your feelings. We do have difficulties with expressing feelings in our culture – mainly because, not being used to doing so, we often can't even put a name to our own feelings. Reasoning with our kids – that is, trying to find a solution to disagreements through talking – doesn't mean you always have to be reasonable. Feelings are very rarely amenable to cold logic and if you are trying to reach an agreement and understanding over something that is striking an emotional cord, but trying to do it in an unemotional way, the message will be mixed and therefore dishonest.

Paula found herself getting upset whenever her teenagers appeared to waste food. They had endless arguments over this, usually beginning like this:

Paula Adam, will you please not leave the crusts and the lettuce leaves when I make you a sandwich. Think of all the starving children in India!

Adam Well, send the bloody crusts to the starving children in India, then.

Having learnt about 'I' messages, she started to use them:

Paula Will you please not leave the crusts and the lettuce leaves when I make you a sandwich. I keep thinking of all the starving children in India and that makes me really upset.

Adam Well, send a donation to Oxfam and they'll send some crusts and lettuce all of their own to the starving children in India!

Paula realised that she still wasn't actually sending an 'I' message. So she dug deep into her own feelings to find the genuine emotion she had when her children didn't eat her food. She realised that, like many of us, she wasn't exactly sure at first what emotion she had been experiencing. Difficulties in communication often come about because we say one thing and mean another. How can your teens take your concern over the starving children in India, when, deep down, they know only too well that this isn't the reason for your outburst? And how can you sort out your misunderstandings unless you can identify what you really do feel? To get in touch with her feelings, Paula used a feelings exercise like the one opposite.

Digging down deeper

When she had done such an exercise Paula realised her emotion wasn't upset, it was panic. The panic, she eventually realised, that her own mother had installed in her whenever she refused food. Her mother had been a war baby and the sight of wasted food aroused anger and genuine fear, with memories of going hungry and never knowing where the next meal was coming from. She had passed this dreadful uncertainty onto Paula, who had felt guilty every time she left a meal unfinished. So next time, she tried this:

Paula You know, Gran used to make me feel dreadful whenever I left food and that's why I get in a panic when you do, too.

Adam OK, Mum, but you're not Gran and I'm not you.

Exercise: **touching on feelings**

Do this exercise with another adult you can trust. Most of us do find it hard, and often frightening, to get in touch with emotions. That doesn't only apply to the painful emotions such as fear or anger. It also means that we sometimes hold love, happiness and joy at bay. After all, once we let the barriers down to one we may be overwhelmed by all of them. Doing this exercise may be surprisingly powerful so do it when you feel safe and secure, with someone you care about and trust.

Have a look at this list of emotions. How many of them strike a chord with you? Are they feelings from the present or the past? Are there any you feel, but call by another name? Are there some you find too scary to be comfortable in feeling?

Joy
Stress
Coldness
Pleasure
Incompetence
Calm
Lust
Misery
Boredom
Foolishness
Love
Panic
Worry

Happiness
Inadequacy
Hate
Warmth
Despair
Contempt
Satisfaction
Grief
Peace
Disgust
Sympathy
Amusement

Are there any others you'd like to add to the list?

Paula needed the final step in getting feelings across, which is to be congruent. Being congruent is matching the outward message to the inward feeling, and so not sending a mixed and unclear message. For a variety of reasons, even when we do know how we truly feel we tend to mute the messages we send other people. Either we want to be polite, or we don't want to scare the person with our feelings, or we're embarrassed about the way we feel. Paula realised her emotional reaction had been so strong that she had been trying to hide it. She felt panic, but it came out as mild reproof. A good formula to use when being congruent is, 'When you (do so-and-so) I feel (this emotion) because (this is the reason I feel it) so please (this is what I would like you to do).' And as you say it, let the emotion show!

Paula Adam, when you leave food I really feel panic-y and upset, because Gran used to make me feel dreadful when I did that. Please, could you tell me when you don't want salad so I can leave it out of the sandwich.

Adam Sorry, Mum, I didn't realise it hurt you so much. I'll tell you in future, OK?

Picking the moment

It's important to pick and choose the situations over which you want to disagree. You'll 'win' more often if the battle is about something you have good reason to want to insist upon. Something, in other words, about which you might reasonably ask them to agree or compromise over. The more fights you have over trivia or your personal taste as opposed to theirs, the more often you will get tied up in destructive and futile arguments. If you keep the times you want to say no to the few occasions when you feel strongly, they are more likely to respect your point of view and come around with good grace.

Exercise: **acceptance or change**

When you and your teen aren't getting on, every little annoyance can blow up into a grand stand-up row. The trick is to save disputes for the important things – and to make those fights constructive discussions rather than conflicts. Try this exercise to work out your priorities.

- What are the things you seriously dislike about your teen?
- What are the things that just get on your nerves?
- And what are the things you actually like?

Draw up three columns using these headings:

This makes me angry
This annoys me
This pleases me.

Think of them as the three colours of a traffic light. Red is the STOP sign; something you'd really like your teenager to change. Yellow is WARNING; something that puts you on edge, that they should be aware about. And Green is GO; something you really like and they might think about doing more, as a way of getting the balance right. Fill in the columns and talk over what you've written with your partner or a friend. Why do these come to mind? Can you think about earlier times when these things have pleased or annoyed you? Of what does it remind you when your teen does them?

Think of the relationships in a family as a piggy bank. Each time you have a row – and make an entry in the red or yellow column – you take out a coin. If you are forever taking out, pretty soon the bank is empty and you have nothing left. But every time you put in a coin – by making an entry in the green column – you fill up the bank. Having disputes does less harm to family harmony if you keep filling the bank as well as taking away.

Having a constructive argument

There's nothing wrong with having a disagreement. The problems arise when it just leads to shouting, anger and further confusion. If someone is being accused of nagging, a common complaint in arguments, the chances are that their request is not being heard, either because the other person doesn't want to hear, they aren't making themselves clear or because the real demand is concealed. The trick is to make sure you are being heard and that you make yourself clear. The next time there is an issue in your home, set about tackling it in the following way.

Sit down with your teenager. Agree a set time for your discussion, so that you will spend the next 30 minutes, or whatever, talking it over together. Or agree to talk until both of you think you have arrived at some conclusion. Use a clock to make sure both of you get an equal share of speaking and being heard, and listening. Also use the following guidelines.

Using 'I'

When you talk about what is bothering you, you have to say 'I'. It's supposed to be arrogant or selfish to use the 'I' word so we tend to be brought up to avoid it. When we want to make a point, in discussion or argument, we either claim 'Everyone' or 'All my friends' or 'Your father/mother' thinks so and so, rather than taking responsibility for those feelings ourselves. Or we put the responsibility on the other person, by saying 'You make me think or do such and such'. One important step to constructive arguing is owning, or taking responsibility for, our own feelings. So, using 'You', 'One', 'They', 'Everyone' – in fact anything except 'I' is outlawed. There is a great difference to saying, 'I'm angry because you don't tidy up the living room when you said you would and that makes me feel you don't listen to me' instead of 'You're lazy, selfish and inconsiderate!' The main difference is that the other person might rightly object to being called names, especially when they might have had a reason for what happened. Once they disagree you will find yourself stuck in the circular argument. But no one can disagree with an honest explanation of your own feelings. And once they are explained, you may be well on your way to dealing with them.

Confronting problems, not people

The argument should not be about them, but what they do. When you feel upset, stop to work out exactly what is bothering you. Instead of shouting at the person, explain what your anger or upset is really about, then find a way of agreeing on a resolution.

Accepting what needs to be done

Accept that you can't help what you feel, only what you do about it. As we have already discussed, anyone in a family is likely to have a complex and mixed range of feelings about themselves, the other people involved and the situation. Perhaps one of the most important messages we need to take on board is that those feelings, however destructive they are and however much they may distress you, are likely to be natural and normal. If you want to become comfortable with yourself and to reach a working arrangement with everyone else, the first step is to recognise and understand why you feel the way you do. So accept your feelings, even if they are sometimes ones you would rather not own to. Be honest about what you are feeling and why. You are not to blame for your emotions.

Taking control

Accept that you are, however, in control of the actions you take because of your emotions. You are being dishonest if you say you can't help what you might do.

Having gained some insight into why having a teenager in the family might be so difficult, you can pinpoint your own fears, angers or anxieties and come to understand how the other people involved might feel, and then work on strategies for making a change. Sometimes a 'pre-emptive strike' can nip problems in the bud before they really begin. Many families start off the teenage years badly or go through difficult periods, so don't despair. There are many things you can all do to improve your life together.

Take the It Test

If an argument is brewing, step back, bite your tongue and lower your voice. What often happens when we feel angry or challenged is that all our body language moves towards having a fight. We look away from the person, refusing eye contact and so say that we don't want to talk this over. Or we stare at them in such a way as to try to force them to back down. Our fists may ball up, our body becomes tense and we may stand up or step forward, taking their space and emphasising our size and authority. When we speak, our voice becomes loud and strident. We may stress what we say by jabbing a forefinger at them – a very attacking gesture. Next time the temperature rises, try the IT TEST – Invite, Talk, Time out, Explain, Stand your ground and Treat yourself.

Invite

Defuse what is happening by becoming aware of your feelings and the way you are showing them. Instead of pointing a finger, hold up both palms as if to say 'Peace! We don't want to fight.' Invite the other person to sit down with you and get on their wavelength, to sort this out together.

Talk

Talk it over. Banish from your vocabulary the phrases 'Because I say so', 'Do as I say' , 'We're doing it my way or not at all', or anything else that closes the conversation. However unrealistic or unreasonable you think your teen is being, invite them to make their case and listen to them, and then ask them to hear you out too. Seek a solution that meets with both your approval, however unfeasible finding one might seem at first. Don't forget Sherlock Holmes! 'Eliminate the impossible and whatever remains, however improbable, must be the truth.' Substitute answer for truth, and go for it.

Time out

We all tend to want an instant answer and young people above all want it and want it NOW. If you're not sure or need time to consider, don't be rail-roaded into making a snap decision. Ask for a time out to consider – but do not, under any circumstances, make this an excuse to try to brush the whole subject under the carpet. Give them a specific time when you can talk about this again, and use the delay to think it over and talk about it further.

Explain

Make a point of becoming very clear about what it is that you want and what it might be that upsets you. It is unfair, for instance, to work yourself up into a rage and accuse your teens of not tidying their room when (a) they've put dirty clothes in the laundry basket and brought the coffee cups downstairs, but haven't used the vacuum cleaner because that's the way they like it, or (b) you didn't tell them you wanted it done today and they really were going to do it at the weekend. If, instead of just saying 'Clean up your room', you'd said, 'I'd like you to clean your room, but shall we go over what I would like you to do? And I do want you to do it by tomorrow evening – is that OK?' Define, explain and negotiate what are your requests and needs, and listen to their feelings on the matter, too.

Stand your ground

Don't be deflected or put off. Persist in spite of their odd looks, jeers, suspicion or hostility to trying a new way of working together. You may find there is an initial increase in tears and anger when you change your way of dealing with your family. You may also find it feels uncomfortable, if not weird and unnatural. It takes hard work. Waiting till they finish what they're saying just so you can butt in to say your pre-prepared speech is far easier than concentrating on listening to and hearing them! But the old ways don't work, so it's worth trying these out, however hard – in practice and on your self-image – they may be.

❝I was trying so hard to use the lessons I'd learnt at a parenting class. I was reflecting and using "I messages", and all I seemed to get was, "Don't you come the counsellor with me! You're only doing this because you learnt it at those bloody classes. I don't want to be a guinea pig for your lessons, thank you very much." One day, it just got all too much and I burst into tears. I said I was really trying to do the right thing and be a better mother, and help all of us have a better time. I said it hurt me when he was so dismissive when I wanted to get it right. I said I wasn't trying to trick him or get one over him, I wanted to do the right thing. There was this awful silence. Then he mumbled Sorry and left the room. We never mentioned it again, but ever since then our relationship has improved beyond all recognition. He listens to me and, best of all, trusts me to listen to him. **9**

Treat yourself

What stops you communicating with your kids is often leftover feelings of resentment, anger and lack of self-worth from your own childhood. If you want them to value you, and value themselves, the first step is to value yourself. Give yourself time off every now and then. After a hard day, take a break with a treat that's just for you. It may be an uninterrupted hour with the music or television or radio programme of your choice. Or a soak in a hot bath, with a book and a drink. Or a glass of wine or beer with your feet up and the newspaper or a magazine. Claim time out with a companion, to do adult things in adult time.

Trust your teens to mean well even if or when they don't do well. Young people have their own needs and wishes, and their own interests at heart, just as adults do. But the fact is that most of us would rather co-operate and get along, and care for each other, too, than ride roughshod over other people and not give a damn for how they feel. Most young people actually largely agree with their parent's ideas and values – it's the details and the style that may differ, not the essentials. When, however, young people never get their own needs met is the time that they can become demanding, insistent and self-ish. If you want to make limits and make them stick, sometimes you need to think laterally. If you keep finding yourself wondering why your young people keep pushing the boundaries it may be that you should move the boundary. Co-operation is a far better tool than obedience, which is why rewards work rather better than punishment, praise than blame.

Discipline: crime and punishment

Teens need to learn how to behave for their own and it's own sake, not just to do as you tell them. If you want to enlist their co-operation, discuss how much this may be for their happiness not your convenience – and if you're having battles, perhaps the reason is that it is your wishes and convenience you're regarding more than their well-being. Is your attention a reward for bad or good behaviour? If they've learned the only time they do and the only way they can get your attention is by acting up, that's what they'll do. Positive discipline, where you thank them, appreciate them and tell them you love them, focuses on positive behaviour; expects it, looks for it, rewards it, fosters it. Negative discipline, where you object to what they do and say, complain about their behaviour, actually reinforces all those things you hate.

Positive discipline

Discipline in this form:

- Takes account of young people's as well as adults' feelings: 'I can understand you felt upset and had a right to feel angry. I just don't like it when you leave the room and slam the door.'
- Encourages teens to take responsibility for their own behaviour: 'It must be disappointing for you that your favourite sweatshirt is dirty but it is up to you to put it in the laundry basket.'
- Allows them to share decisions: 'I liked the way you came up with a plan for discussing our Easter holiday. We seem to have a disagreement about this weekend so how shall we resolve it?'
- Has self-discipline as its aim: 'I know you have to finish that homework before the end of the holidays. If you want any help, please ask, but now I know you're aware

of what you have to do, I'll leave you to decide when you'll do it.'

Force

Force as a method of enforcing your wishes is a poor choice when you're dealing with young children, and worse than useless when applied to teens. This form of discipline:

- Teaches kids might is right. If you, who are stronger, bigger and have more authority than they do, are justified in making them do what you want, that logically means they can apply the same test too. When they are stronger, bigger and have more authority, either when dealing with younger children or when they grow up, they too can throw their weight about.
- Makes them too angry and humiliated to reflect on what they did wrong. When you enforce your point of view, even when their actions were wrong, a power-play simply leaves them thinking about your use of strength. All they will think about is their own embarrassment and an intense desire to get back at you or make you feel what they are feeling.
- Doesn't give anyone space to put it right. Punishment has a way of wiping out the offence. Hit a young person for bullying, lying, playing truant and why should they make amends or change their ways? Your action has wiped the slate clean – until next time, when you are right back where you started.
- Escalates. Hit out, and where do you go from there? Hitting harder? Punishing more?
- Builds up resentment and has a time limit. Use smacking as your method of disciplining your children and one of these days you'll find they have the size or strength to hit back. And since you demonstrated a lack of respect for their personal space and integrity by hitting them, they may display the same to you.

We often punish our children, of whatever age, because we are scared of what will happen if we don't. We think that not applying limits will mean they get out of control. Or we believe that we will have failed as parents if we don't draw firm lines. But, the main problem with punishment as a tool to help young people become socialised is that it doesn't work. What should we do instead? We could try problem solving.

Problem solving

When you hit a point of disagreement or conflict, the first thing you need is calm. Call a time out and agree you'll work through the following six-point plan.

1 Focus on what they need

Young people need flexibility and to be allowed to rebel, but they also need rules, consistency and structure. The trick is to make these something that has their agreement and understanding. Say, 'These are the rules, take it or leave it', and they'll probably leave them! A system that runs on negatives – don't do this, no doing that, you shouldn't, mustn't, can't – is far less likely to be effective than one that has positive values as its basis. Focusing on pointing out what they did right, rather than what they did wrong and asking them to do what you want rather than what you don't want is far more likely to get the goods.

It is also important to be generally affirming about our young people. Don't only praise or thank them for specific actions, when they've done something. When anyone only gets 'a stroke' after particular events, their self-esteem becomes tied to activity. They get the idea that they must do something to please you and that your pleasure is dependent on their fulfilling tasks or actions.

Instead of an overall sense of self-worth, they will only feel good about themselves when getting praise and be dependent on other people's view of them, not on their own self-image.

Young people need our time and attention, our good regard and praise – but praise for themselves, not ourselves. Parents frequently bask in the congratulations and admiration of other people for their children, as if nothing the young person does or is, is by their own efforts; it's all down to us. We may be proud of our kids and we may have good reason to feel we have a lot to do with their achievements, but let them take the credit for themselves. Being proud of them too often comes across as pride of ownership – as if it's we who should take the praise for what ever they've done, not them. Being proud for them puts the achievement where it belongs – in their hands.

❝I can't tell you how much it has always made my blood boil to have my mother introduce me and say "Didn't I do a good job?" The things I'm most pleased and proud about myself are things I've really had to work out for myself, often in the teeth of her objections and manipulation, so she didn't do at all a good job and it's most unfair to try to claim the credit. Of course, I do understand what it's all about. She feels she was a lousy mother – she was a lousy mother – and she's desperate for me and anyone else to forgive her and say she is all right. But that isn't the way to do it and it more than infuriates me, and always has. In fact, if she'd only stop and let me be myself, she and I may be able to build a better relationship. As it is, ever since I was 13 years old we've been at loggerheads. ❞

Let young people own their own body. It can be hard, as a parent, to see or accept the boundary that separates us and our children. After all, what seems to be just a few scant years ago, they were a twinkle in our own eyes and then tiny specks of our own bodies. For nine months, they occupied their mother's body and it can be very difficult to let go that sense of connection, of their being an extension and a part of us. This shows in what may seem, to the adult saying it, as joking or loving remarks and habits. 'Put a sweater on, I'm feeling cold!' may seem a harmless and affectionate bit of family banter, but what it also says is that you think you speak for them, answer for them and can act for them. 'Paul wants to be an astronaut', 'Mum I haven't wanted to be an astronaut since I was 5!', 'Don't contradict your mother, Paul!', or, 'She takes sugar in her coffee' – 'Dad, I'm not dumb and I've been having my coffee black without sugar for ages', 'Don't be cheeky!' None of these may matter individually but they add up and deny teens their own feelings, thoughts and choices.

Young people need privacy. Reading their diaries or listening in to phone calls, discussing them with their teachers or others behind their backs, only underlines that you don't trust or respect them or feel that they are capable of making decisions or choices. Encourage their autonomy and show respect for if they're having a hard time. They are far more likely to come to you for help and support if you've given them the chance to try on their own than if you won't let go.

Of course, finding out what they need calls for all your listening skills. Asking too many questions is often felt as intrusive and controlling. You can show an interest without it being an interrogation, with openers, reflective and active listening.

2 Consider your own feelings

Accept that anyone will hate to be made redundant and when we acknowledge their freedom, that is what we may be doing. If you are going to succeed in letting go, not discouraging them and not rushing to answer all their questions and fix all their problems for them, you need to feel needed, wanted, essential in other parts of your life. Parents often feel guilty about doing things for themselves, feeling that it deprives their children and makes them selfish and bad parents. In fact, the more you are able to take your own feelings and needs into account, the more you may be able to give your teens what they really need from you.

3 Brainstorm

Brainstorming is a game or technique that really helps you solve problems and come up with solutions. It has the added bonus of giving participants a good laugh and drawing people together. Try this exercise for a quick demonstration of how it works. Get a sheet of paper, give yourself five minutes and write down as many uses as you can think for a plastic drinking straw. Go!

Done? Did you think of using it as a hairpin, or a piece of jewellery, or a quill pen? What about as an automatic pot plant watering device, or half of a pair of chopsticks or a gambling chip for a game of poker? Some of the ideas you might have come up with would be sensible and practical, some might work and some would be fanciful. The point about brainstorming is that sometimes, when we let our imaginations run riot, we find that the most unlikely solutions could work.

In a brainstorming session, everyone is allowed their say and no idea is out of bounds. Elect one member of your group to be the recorder and another to be time-keeper. The recorder lays out a large sheet of paper. Explain the problem – you need a way, say, of stopping the arguments about what time your teenagers come home on Saturday nights. It is important to be clear about the problem. If you are vague, contradictory or are only seeing the difficulty from one point of view, you may find it harder to reach a resolution. Saying you want a way of enforcing gating hours, for instance, is unlikely to

get much co-operation from our teens! Since the real
problem, most of the time, is the argument caused by
your difference of opinion, focus on that. ANY solutions
can then be put forward.

Set yourself a time: 20 minutes is usually enough to get
the creative juices going but not so much that people
run out of steam. At this stage, what is most important is
that the solutions need not be sensible, workable or even
desirable. Get every single person to jump in with as
many ideas as they can, and write every single one of
them down WITHOUT COMMENT. 'Let us stay out all
night', 'Stop worrying', 'Put them in leg irons', 'Send a
chauffeur driven limo'. At this point, every solution
should be recorded, with no criticism or complaint.

The recorder should function also as a facilitator,
pulling anyone up who pours cold water on anyone for
their remarks or tries to discuss them at this juncture.
You'll find out why silly suggestions are welcome in brainstorming when you go on to the next stage.

Once the time limit is up and you've put all your ideas
down, take a break. Then, start at the top of your list and
talk each one over. Don't dismiss anything out of hand,
but do ask everyone what they think about it. Why not, in
this instance, accept the 'Stop worrying' solution? Think
about it and then explain why you'd find this hard or
impossible. Explaining your point of view allows you to
think it over – there is just an outside possibility they
might be right – or gives you the chance to have them listen to how you feel. Chauffeur-driven limos may be out
of the question, but what about money for a taxi? Staying
out all night may be unacceptable, but if half the problem is that they go out with friends who live a long way
away, why not let them stay the night with them?

The key to brainstorming is that, hidden among all
the jokes, dross and rubbish, you are likely to find a gem
you might otherwise not have discovered. Done properly,
it also allows the whole family the chance to feel brought

together in the search for a solution. Young people can be responsible, caring and sensible – if allowed to be so. The final benefit is that a solution that had been genuinely created and agreed to by everyone becomes theirs. Most of us want to kick against rules that have been imposed upon us from above. When the solution is something we have had some input into knowing is necessary, we 'own' it. It's our rule and we have a vested interest in making it work.

Brainstorming works because:

- Everyone has, and everyone knows they have, as much right to speak out as anyone else
- Everyone has, and everyone knows they have, as much chance of having their solution taken seriously as anyone else
- It's fun
- It helps you think of difficulties as challenges that can be overcome, not problems that can't be solved.

4 Have a family round table discussion

Adults often use 'family discussions' as a way of telling children what they have decided to do. It isn't, however, a true family round table unless you listen as much, if not more, than you talk and unless young people are given as much space and respect to have their say as are adults. Round table talks may not always be what you need. There will be plenty of times when simply having the time and space to talk with and listen to someone else in the family is important. Try to make a point of allowing every member of the family some time to simply talk and be heard by you and by the other adults. But a family parliament is an ideal way, not just of keeping in touch, but also of pulling everyone together. It is, above all, a good technique to try if you are having problems and need to clear the air and one that, if used regularly, can head off disagreements. If you feel that teenagers are too young to give their views, or that you are uncomfortable about listening to them, this may be a difficult exercise for you to become accustomed to. It may seem false or awkward to think about sitting round a table actually explaining your views or listening to someone else's, but however silly all this sounds, the fact is that it can be enormously helpful.

The difference between a dictatorship and a democracy is the assembly. In the days when city states were small, all the members entitled to vote would come together to voice their opinions and vote. As populations became bigger, those with a vote would use it to put their choice of elected member into a senate or parliament, to discuss and legislate. You can run your family as a dictatorship, where only adults have a say, or you can claim you're presiding over a democracy where your kids are too young to be able to make choices. If you do, don't forget what usually happens in such systems. The oppressed peoples either overthrow the state in bloody revolution, or emigrate and never come back! There are three main rules to make a Family Round Table discussion work.

Owning what you say: the most important rule is that everyone has to 'own' what they say. That means, everything you put forward has to be your own thoughts and feelings and you should acknowledge them as such, using 'I think' or 'I feel'. No one can say, 'So-and-so says', or, 'Everyone knows', or talk about what other people do or what you think they think. You can talk about how other people's behaviour affects you, by saying, 'When you do such-and-such, I feel . . .', but the aim is to put your point of view, not to criticise or attack other people. Remember, the key is confronting problems, not people.

Equality: everyone, from oldest to youngest, is to have an equal turn to speak and to be heard. You might like to go round the table letting each person say one thing, to start. Then take turns to add to the discussion. You can use an object handed round to signify whose turn it is to speak and ask everyone to keep the rule about only talking when they have had it handed on to them. It helps to appoint one person to act as the 'Facilitator' for a family round table, and to have each member of the group take it turn-and-turn about to play this role. The facilitator ensures that everyone takes it in turns to speak and not interrupt.

Consensus: the eventual aim of your discussion is to find a space where everyone feels they have been heard and appreciated, and have heard and appreciated everyone else's point of view. There should be no winners or losers, but an all-round agreement on the outcome. To that end, no one is to be shouted down for what they say. Discuss the points rather than arguing with the person. Set aside time for the discussion and allow everyone a chance to speak, as many times as they like.

5 Draw up a contract

Having brainstormed and discussed, you need a clear way of keeping track of what you agreed needed changing and how you've agreed to go about it. To do that, you should draw up a contract.

The idea is to write down exactly what everyone has said they will do. The key is that it shouldn't be one-sided, with one person or a few people asked to make an effort or make changes and other people acting as usual. Work out a fair exchange and one on which you can all agree. Make a precise record, including:

- What you've all agreed to do
- How you agree to do it
- When you agree to do it by
- For how long you have agreed to do this.

Everyone should sign the contract, and have a copy for themselves. The original should be pinned up on the Bulletin Board.

6 Follow up

Review the contract and the agreed changes regularly. If the terms are not being met, discuss why and whether the contract needs to be redrawn or whether something needs to be adjusted.

There are several very good spin-offs to this form of discussion. One is that it means you no longer have to be – you no longer should be – in the position of policing your family. If two or more of your children have an argument, they should bring it to the round table discussion. But it's their responsibility, not yours, to sort out. If one of the younger members of the family and an adult have a disagreement, it's up to the ones involved to settle it, not the role of one adult alone. This puts a stop to Mum feeling she has to mediate between Dad and his children, when he should be having his own dialogue with them. Or Dad being cast in the role of disciplinarian when the argument may be between Mum and teen and over something they disagree about and he doesn't. Another benefit is that if agreed changes are not fulfilled, you have every right to insist.

Broken Record

A useful technique for putting your foot down, when it's justified, is Broken Record. Even when you do it 'right', you may not get the 'right' response. Young people, after all, are not robots and won't run the intended programme just because we seem to push the correct buttons. They have their own thoughts and agendas, and may need some time to see in what ways they too may benefit from this new style of parenting. If you're coming up against arguments for arguments' sake or if your teens are just dragging their heels, don't allow yourself to be diverted or drawn into arguments, just be insistent. Keys to Broken Record are:

- Saying something that shows you've heard and recognise what your teenager is saying to you and sympathise; I can see . . . , you say . . . , I realise . . . , that may be how it feels to you . . .
- Being clear about what you want done
- Not losing your temper
- Standing your ground.

Paula Adam, you agreed to tidy this room up by the time I got home and it's not been done. Please do it while I make tea.

Adam Oh, Mum, I'm busy now.

Paula I can see you have things you want to do, but I'd like you to tidy the room now.

Adam I'll do it after tea.

Paula You say you'll do it after tea, but I'd like you to do it now please.

Adam You're always nagging me!

Paula I can see how you might feel I'm getting at you, but please, I want you to tidy the room now.

Adam God, you're just doing this counsellor thing at me again and I hate it!

Paula That may be how it feels to you, but I'd like you to tidy this room please.

Adam Mum, I've had a really hard day. Can't I just have a few minutes peace and then I'll do it.

Paula I realise you've had a rough day. Please tidy this room up now.

Adam OK, OK, I'm doing it.

Be polite, don't raise your voice or lose your temper. Persist, repeating the request and go on far longer than you might think would be comfortable. If you keep it calm and don't rise to any bait or argument, you will be surprised how many times you can simply repeat a message. If you're not getting anywhere, after as many attempts as you feel able to repeat, try one final time.

Paula I've asked you ten times and I'd like to ask you once more to please tidy this room now.

If you then feel you are getting nowhere or are losing your cool, break off saying:

Paula OK, we'll leave this for ten minutes and then we'll discuss it again.

Go away and congratulate yourself for not having lost your temper and for having left the door open for further talk. After ten minutes, go back. You may find your teenager has started doing what you asked – if so, say thank you but make no further comment. If not, resume and continue. If you do this without reproaches, complaint or threats and without getting hooked into arguing, it isn't nagging. It's making yourself clear. Your teen will get the message that you're serious, won't be deflected, drawn or incited to violence (verbal or otherwise) and will persist. Sooner or later, they are likely to co-operate.

Modelling

Whatever you want from your teenagers – respect, attention, consideration – you have to give them first. Young people learn best by example and as a matter of simple justice, are owed as much as we wish them to give us. If you're asking them to fix something, you might like to turn the spotlight on yourself and your life too. 'Do as I say, not as I do' is possibly the very worst motto for family life – the TOTAL PITS, in fact!

Young people have little power. The only way they can make their feelings heard is by shouting, screaming, sulking and crying – and when they do any of this, we tell them they're being unreasonable. Without realising it there is a whole range of belittling and argumentative patterns that we fall into that will inevitably drive an interaction with your teenager into a confrontation. If you look at this scenario between Paula and her sons Adam and Joe you can see how it led, step by step, into being a stand-up shouting match.

Paula has come home from work to find her two sons in the kitchen, making themselves a sandwich after school.

	What they said	What they felt	What they thought	How it came over
Paula	*This place is a mess. Now look what you made me do – I've broken this mug and it's all your fault.*	Tired, angry and disappointed.	Oh no, what a mess and after the day I've had. I just wanted a few minutes peace!	Blaming and accusing.
Adam	*No I didn't, I only wanted something to eat.*	Shocked, hurt and surprised.	She's only been in a second and she's on at us. We live here too, can't we help ourselves to a snack? It's not my fault she's clumsy!	Sullen and refusing to take responsibility for the mess.
Paula	*You're so lazy and selfish, I'm fed up with you both. Tidy this place up or you're going to be sorry.*	Annoyed and exasperated.	They're going to leave me to tidy up after them, like they always do. I can't get them to pay the slightest attention to me.	Name calling/labelling the person. Threatening.
Adam	*OK, OK, just give us a chance!*	Got at and powerless.	If we'd tried, she'd still be on at us, so what's the point?	Argumentative and rude.

	What they said	What they felt	What they thought	How it came over
Paula	*Don't talk back to me in that way. In my day, young man, children knew to keep a civil tongue in their heads. Young people today are so rude.*	Affronted and hurt.	Why do they talk to me like that? Don't they realise I'm doing this for their good?	Lecturing and moralising.
Joe	*Oh come on Mum, you'd think we were trashing the place the way you go on.*	Embarrassed and confused.	Why does there always have to be a row? Are we really that bad?	Evasive and whining.
Paula	*All right, all right, you run along. I'll clean the place up and then I'll make dinner. I'd rather do the job myself then I know it'll be done properly. No, leave that, leave it all.*	Put upon.	I might as well do it myself or it won't get done properly.	Martyrdom.
Joe	*Well, if that's how you feel.*	Dismissed and disregarded.	There's no point in trying, my best is never good enough for her.	Ungrateful and callous.

	What they said	**What they felt**	**What they thought**	**How it came over**
Paula	*Yes I do! Go and do your homework. Your room needs tidying too. Why do I have to ask you again and again?*	Unvalued.	He doesn't listen to a word I say and if I don't tell him what to do, he'd never get anything done.	Commanding and badgering.
Joe	*God, why don't you get off my case!*	Angry and hurt.	All she ever does is nag, nag, nag.	Aggressive.
Paula	*Why can't you be like that nice boy next door? I bet he never talks back to his parents!*	Despairing.	Why do we always have to fight? Why can't it be different?	Making comparisons.
Paula (as Adam comes back, dressed up to go out to see his friends)	*Oh, don't you look nice, I don't think. I'm sure everyone's going to be really impressed and those shoes look absolutely perfect with that get-up.*	Shown up.	He looks such a mess, everyone will think I'm a terrible mother and don't look after them properly.	Sarcastic and critical.
Adam	*It's what everyone wears. You don't know anything.*	Self-conscious and picked on.	She never likes what I look like.	Scornful.
Paula	*Oh, well, I suppose that girl I've seen you out with will like it, don't you agree* (cont. overleaf)	Wanting to make amends.	He is growing up and soon he won't be my little boy any more.	Teasing and putting down.

	What they said	What they felt	What they thought	How it came over
	Joe? Adam's been acting quite the little lovebird, or so I've been told. Come on, Adam, tell us what she sees in you. Who's love's young dream, eh?			
Adam	*I've had it! You're always on at me! I'm going out and you can stuff your lousy dinner!*	Humiliated and embarrassed.	Why does she have to make fun of me?	Furious.
Paula (as Adam leaves)	*Well, what was that about? Oh for heaven's sake, Joe, I asked you to clean up not make it worse. You've done it all wrong.*	Awkward.	Why did Adam react like that? He has no right to be angry with me, now I feel like a fool so I'll take it out on Joe.	Fault finding and carping.
Joe	*Look, I've done my best!*	Hopeless.	There's no point in trying, I can never get it right.	Argumentative.
Paula	*Well, of course, I suppose I shouldn't expect any better from you.*	Defensive and dismissive.	Nothing I say ever makes a difference, they're so clumsy and lazy.	Belittling and putting down.

	What they said	What they felt	What they thought	How it came over
Paula (as neighbour comes in)	*Hello Sue, just look at the mess these boys have made of this.*	Caught out.	Oh, no, now Sue will see what a mess my home is in and think badly of me. It's all my fault!	Scornful.
Joe	*Oh, Mum!*	Humiliated.	Why does she have to make a fool of me in front of someone else?	Livid and refusing to take the blame.
Paula	*Yes, well, your father has a point. Neither of you will never be any good at anything. You're a waste of space and time.*	At the end of her tether.	I can't take much more of this.	Giving up on them, 'You'll never be any good'.
Joe	*Christ, I can't do a thing right here. I'm off and to hell with it!*	The last straw.	There's no point in trying.	Having a tantrum.

You could play that entire scenario over again, but this time with Paula making use of communication skills to make it a discussion rather than an argument.

	What they said	What they felt	What they thought	How it came over
Paula	*Hello boys. Oh, I've had a terrible day, am I glad to get home. Let me make myself a cuppa – oh, damn there goes the bloody mug. My fault, leave it there. I'll clean it up when you've put your stuff away. Look, let me have a few minutes to catch my breath and then I'd love to hear what sort of a day you've had.*	Tired and fed up.	Oh no, what a mess and after the day I've had. But I know they'll clear up – especially with a hint!	Hassled but it wasn't their fault. She trusts them to do the right thing.
Adam	*Hi, Mum. You look rough. Don't worry, we'll tidy this in a minute – want a tea?*	Caught out but not blamed.	Poor old Mum, she does take on. We'll get this out the way!	Co-operative.
Paula	*That would be lovely, thank you. I would like the place clean for when I come to make dinner.*	A little apprehensive.	They can be a pain in the butt but I do like my boys.	Appreciative and trusting.
Adam	*OK, OK, just give us a chance!*	Reminded.	I see her point.	Reasonable and joking.
Paula	*Are either of you going out to see friends tonight? I'm making a casserole so it can wait till later, as long as I know.*	No worries.	Two for dinner, three or four?	Just checking.

	What they said	**What they felt**	**What they thought**	**How it came over**
Adam	*I'm going over to Tom's for an hour if that's OK.*	Looking forward to seeing his friends.	Whoops! Nearly forgot to tell her!	Clear and up-front.
Paula	*All right, you run along when you've done your chores. (later) Thanks, I feel really pleased when you do the jobs we've agreed.*	Confident in her sons.	They do live up to my expectations.	Positive.
Joe	*Well, thanks, I'm glad you think so.*	Accepted and approved of.	When I make an effort, she always appreciates it.	Pleased.
Paula	*Yes I do! Are you going to do your homework now or later?*	Valued and acknowledged.	What I say and think of him matters to him. He does try to please me.	Accepting.
Joe	*Oh, I'll go and do it now, then I've got the weekend free.*	On his toes.	I know what she means – do it now! But she's right!	Amused but forgiving.
Paula (Adam comes back, dressed to go out to see his friends).	*Wow! I'm out of date, is that the fashion? Still, I shouldn't talk, you should see what me and your Dad used to wear when we were your age. Remind (cont. overleaf)*	Amazed.	He looks original, but aren't teenage fashions such fun?	You're OK by me.

	What they said	What they felt	What they thought	How it came over
	me to show you our photos some time – that should give us all a good laugh!			
Adam	*Yeah, well, it's what everyone wears.*	A bit self-conscious.	All parents are from the dark ages.	Amused and exasperated.
Paula	*Now, that reminds me, was that girl I saw you with last week a new friend? I don't think you've brought her round yet, have you?*	Curious.	He is growing up and soon he won't be my little boy any more.	Affectionate and trusting.
Adam (kisses her and leaves)	*I'm off! See you later!*	A little embarrassed.	Mothers!	Shy.
Paula	*OK, Joe, thanks for clearing up.*	Boys!	He really does make an effort.	Accepting.
Joe	*We like to do our best!*	Pleased.	It feels good when she appreciates me.	Open.
Paula	*Well, of course, I know you always do your best.*	Loving.	What I say makes a difference, so it's important to build him up.	Supportive.

	What they said	What they felt	What they thought	How it came over
Paula (Sue, their neigh-bour, comes in)	*Hello Sue, come and join me and my beautiful boy.*	Welcoming.	Take us as you find us.	Affectionate.
Joe	*Oh, Mum!*	Amused.	There she goes again, but she means well.	Teenage exasperation.
Paula	*Yes, well, you'll just have to put up with the fact I love you and like to make it clear.*	Happy.	Aren't I lucky?	My sons are worthwhile.
Joe	*Christ, I'm out of here!*	Valued.	There's every point in trying.	You're awful, but I like it.

Role reversal

We need to learn how to appreciate, thank and apologise to our kids. One way of getting on their wavelength and learning to appreciate their point of view is role playing. Teenagers may be growing up, and may indeed have reached a size when they look at us eye-to-eye, but years of looking down on them affects the way we treat them. It's no accident that we use the phrase 'to look down on someone' to mean feeling we know better than them. You find yourself assuming the position of moral superi-or and leader when you are taller and even though this no longer applies, parents still act as if they are the taller,

Family phone answering message: it's not just your home – they live there too!

If you have a phone answering machine, make sure every-one in the family is named on it. There is nothing as disen-franchising as knowing any friend who rings for you may be told your parents live there, but you don't even figure. Get together to record something that represents every-one, including the dog if that's what people want. Naomi and her partner Dane had their daughter record the following message on their answer machine for all the family including Dane's son, Derri. 'Hi, this is Tonya and if you've called to speak to Naomi or Dane you're out of luck cos I haven't the foggiest where they are or what they're doing. I'm probably in my room with the sound turned up and if it was Derri you rang to speak to he may be at his Mum's or he could be in his room. (sound of barking) If it was Jake you wanted then you're really sad, wanting to talk to a dog! Anyway, leave us a message and one of us will get back to you, and who knows, it might even be the right one! Byeee!' If it sounds stupid or naff to you, console yourself with the thought that at least it confirms in all your friends' minds what a cross you have to bear!

bigger and better. It's a salutary lesson to change places for a time.

It can be useful to offer your young people a day or a weekend in which positions in the house are turned upside down. An old proverb does say that you can never understand a person until you walk a mile in their shoes. If you want to know how your teenagers feel about the relationships in your house, have a day in which they play your roles and you play theirs. If you think they would take advantage of this to point score or work off grudges, what are you saying about the way you treat them? If you think that it would be risky and dangerous, negotiate beforehand about rules that could be mutually agreed.

Clearly taking the car and/or emptying the drinks cabinet would be ill advised on their part – but then if they are going to act like adults, which is the point of the exercise, they wouldn't behave irresponsibly anyway, would they?

The aim of the exercise is for them to experience what it may be like to have to organise the family, thinking ahead and making sure there is food in the house and that it gets to the table at the right time, that everyone does their chores and fulfils their responsibilities. And for you to see what it's like to be at the receiving end of being instructed and having to ask permission to see your friends, turn on the television or use the phone. Brainstorm together exactly what you feel you have to do over a weekend and hand over responsibility for that.

Next weekend, role play being with each other as adult to adult. Treat them the same way as you would treat your partner or visitors, consciously dealing with your teenagers as if they were the same age as you, and see how this affects your behaviour and theirs.

Talking to young people about ourselves

We often trap ourselves with our beliefs in parental invulnerability and omnipotence. We feel we need to be seen as strong, capable and all-knowing. We fear that if we show hesitation, weakness or inadequacy in front of our children, one of a variety of disasters will happen. Perhaps we fear that, once called into question, our competency will collapse. Perhaps we think our children will gain the upper hand and take control. Perhaps we fear they will be scared and upset to see us overwhelmed. Whatever, we often resort to techniques that close rather than open communication, instead of inviting it and – as we see it – be caught or even found out. One of the biggest taboos in parent/child interaction is being open and honest about our own feelings. It's a bit like being a conjurer or magician; we feel that if we tell our audience what's going on behind the screen, they'll no longer believe the illusion or respect the practitioner.

Here's a familiar scenario between a teenager and a parent. Sandy has come home after an expensive hour getting the week's shopping at the local supermarket. She finds the phone bill has arrived, and she knows the bill for the final instalment on the family's annual holiday is due any day. Her daughter, Gita, bounces into the kitchen.

	What they said	What they felt	What they thought	How it came over
Gita	*Hi Mum, I need some money.*	Excited, expectant.	Here she is at last!	Careless.
Sandy	*What? Well, that's a nice way to greet me. What's it for?*	Flustered, off-guard, tired.	God, I've only just got in!	Distant, not really listening.
Gita	*I need a pair of leggings.*	Impatient.	I know just what I want – I need to get back before they're all sold!	Demanding.
Sandy	*What's wrong with the ones you've got?*	Apprehensive.	We can't afford it – every penny counts at the moment.	Critical.
Gita	*Oh Mum, they're way out of date. Purleeeease!*	Frustrated.	Why does she always do this?	Whinging.

	What they said	What they felt	What they thought	How it came over
Sandy	*No, you'll have to make do.*	Annoyed.	I haven't had a new pair of leggings for months!	Dismissive.
Gita	*You let Ali have a new sweat shirt last week.*	Angry, hurt.	She doesn't love me as much as Ali.	Argumentative.
Sandy	*Look, we can't afford it! He paid for half out of his paper round and any way he needed that.*	Increasingly upset.	I don't know how we're going to pay for this holiday now.	Aggressive.
Gita	*You never let me have what I want!*	Rejected.	Why does she always give me this nonsense about not affording any-thing. They always seem to find the dosh for the stuff they want!	Querulous.

That didn't feel comfortable, did it? Run the whole encounter again and see if trying it this way might make a difference.

	What they said	What they felt	What they thought	How it came over
Gita	*Hi Mum, I need some money.*	Excited, expectant.	Here she is at last!	Careless.

	What they said	What they felt	What they thought	How it came over
Sandy	*Hello darling, nice to see you too. Just give me a minute to catch my breath and put all this down. Now, what's this all about?*	Flustered, off-guard, tired.	God, I've only just got in! Let's make room to pay attention.	Asking for a brief time-out and then, listening.
Gita	*OK, I need a pair of leggings.*	Impatient.	I know just what I want – I need to get back before they're all sold!	Demanding.
Sandy	*I can see you feel this is important.*	Apprehensive.	We can't afford it – every penny counts at the moment.	Prepared to listen.
Gita	*Well, the thing is, the ones I've got are way out of date. Purleeeease!*	Frustrated.	I have a feeling this isn't going to work.	Wheedling.
Sandy	*Well, let's look at this. I'm worried because we've just had a phone bill and we'll have to pay off the last instalment on the holiday in a few days. We could have a look at the budget and see what's available and what isn't. Do you want to tell me how much they are?*	Concerned.	I'm sure we can come to an understanding – I do know how much being in fashion matters to her.	Receptive.

	What they said	What they felt	What they thought	How it came over
Gita	*The ones I want are £29.99.*	Apprehensive.	Am I asking for too much? I know she'd let me have it if she could.	Upfront.
Sandy	*It's a lot. But I know Ali had a new sweat shirt last week and I'm sure you would like something new, too. He paid for half out of his paper round. Could we agree to leave this till next month, and would you put something towards it, too?*	Understanding.	I do want to be fair.	Offering to negotiate.
Gita	*Thanks, Mum, I know you always listen.*	Mollified.	I suppose money doesn't grow on trees!	Reasonable.

You can see that any exchange goes so much better when everyone explains how they feel. When you can appreciate the other person's feelings and their point of view, several things happen. For a start, much of the anger and aggression of the encounter goes. Even when you don't get exactly what you want, you can at least feel you are being heard and understood. But when it becomes a dialogue, you may find you – and at the same time, the other person – do make gains. Sometimes, the gains are only in being appreciated and heard. Both of you may feel better as a result.

Rights and responsibilities

Where do parental rights stop and child's rights begin?
We tend to operate from the standpoint that parents do
know best for their children and should, therefore, be in
charge in order to guide and protect them. There are
two problems with this. One is that there are occasions
when the parents view of what is best turns out not to be
in the child's interests after all. When adults abuse their
children, this is easy and obvious to spot – but it may happen in more subtle ways, too. When young people grow
up with little ability to be self-determining, a lack of self-
esteem and low self-confidence, it could be said that the
parents concerned may not have achieved their task.
Challenging the idea that parents always know best could
help you to ask for help. If we are able, as a society, to
intervene when we can see that things are going wrong,
fewer children would suffer the extremes of abuse. But
there is a lesser degree of difficulty. Simply by accepting
the theory that parents know best means that we never
listen to kids. More and more we are accepting that
parental rights to control a child do not exist for the benefit of the parent. They exist for the benefit of the child
and they are justified only in so far as they enable the
parent to perform their duties towards the child, and
towards other children in the family. Parental responsibility is the idea that should replace the concept of absolute rights over kids. We need to respect young people's
views, their evolving capacities and growing rights to self-
determination. If we accept that all people should have
the right to identity, physical and personal integrity, freedom of thought, expression, conscience, religion, associ-
ation, privacy and access to information, we need to ask
ourselves, when do you cease to be a child and become a
person?

The Gillick Judgement in the House of Lords in 1986
recognised the concept of parental responsibility rather

than absolute rights. It enshrined in case law the idea that young people have the right to make decisions for themselves once they are considered to be of 'sufficient understanding'. In some Scandinavian countries – notably Finland, Norway and Sweden – children have the same protection under law as adults do. That is, any form of violence and other humiliating or offensive treatment are banned, even when it might be parents or carers meting out the punishment. With marital rape now illegal in the UK, the punishment of children is the only physical assault tolerated in law. The law allows 'reasonable chastisement' and leaves it to parents and the courts to determine what is reasonable. When we're looking at adults, any assault without consent (and some with consent) is an offence, no matter how trivial. We make a distinction in degree or severity – whether it's ABH (actual bodily harm) or GBH (grievous bodily harm) – but it is still an offence. Children have less protection than adults – which means we show them less respect.

What I would like to suggest is a model for family life which makes you partners with your young people, rather than your being in sole charge. See the task as making an alliance, negotiating co-working with all members of a family and working by consensus rather than it being a hierarchical structure run by – and for – parents. One common concern for an idea like this is that it might impose burdens on kids too young to manage such responsibility. But teens do not lack the capacity to be involved in deciding how their own lives can best be run. What, perhaps, you need to separate is self-determination and participation. Being a participant does not mean having to make life and death decisions from day one, simply that views should be heard and taken seriously. Learning to make well-informed choices should be a part of growing up. It doesn't mean you must give them full rights to run their lives until they are capable of being responsible – but how can they learn if not given the chance?

> Being granted respect and having your views valued is the
> way to become a responsible adult

Another concern is that giving young people a say under-
mines the authority of parents and the family. Parents
who themselves have had no experience of being heard
or respected may be loath to give up what they have seen
as hard won power. If you change the way you work – to
listen and liaise – you will feel as if you are losing part of
yourself, your status as an adult and Mum or Dad. On the
contrary, it enhances and strengthens the bonds you
have and the respect you build for each other. Respect
earned and given freely is far greater than respect that is
demanded, 'Because I say so!' Ration out saying 'because
I say so'. It's the joker, so you can only use it once a
game. If you always assume you know best, you'll never
learn anything new. And our kids can teach us so much
that's interesting, exciting and great fun, if only we let
them.

Chapter 5

What to talk about

Ask young people themselves what they want to talk about with their parents or carers, or other adults with whom they come into contact, and they nominate a wide range of subjects. The surprise, to some adults, may be the maturity with which most teens consider such a question. It's not all boy- or girlfriends, partying or music that takes their attention and concern – and even when these are uppermost, there is a serious intent to it, too. The subjects most young people would like to talk over with their parents are family matters, controversial issues such as sex, drink and drugs, emotional, personal and philosophical issues, their future, current affairs – and you, their parents.

Family matters

Top of the list are family matters. Young people want to hear and have the right to have a say about the big decisions that will affect them in their own day-to-day existence. They complain that, all too often, changes such as moving house are conveyed to them as an, 'Oh, by the way . . .'.

Leo is 16-years-old and his parents moved house two years ago:

❛My parents obviously had a reason for moving us from one end of the country to the other so I suppose they thought there was no point in asking us what we thought as it wouldn't have made a difference. But it really made me mad that they never even thought to tell us. We knew something was up but they kept on saying "Nothing" if we asked what was going on and it was my gran who let the cat out of the bag – because she thought we'd already been told. So when we did go back and have it out with them, they made a big deal about how she shouldn't have said anything and they hadn't wanted to worry us, and I'm, like, "Hello, it's us we're talking about here, didn't it occur to you that we might have needed to know?" And the truth is that no, they felt we hadn't needed. They knew best, they were in charge and that was that. There was this girl who I'd just got to know. Maybe it wouldn't have made any difference, but if I'd known a bit earlier that I was being uprooted I'd have held back a bit. As it was, it really hurt to leave her and I'm still not over it. **'**

Parents often want to protect young people from the stress of worrying about 'adult' concerns. We may avoid talking about money problems, concerns over job pressures, serious illness or marital difficulties in front of them. The problem is, that just because there is no open debate, it does not mean that we can successfully hide these matters from them. For a start, they will experience the fall-out – a reduced budget, short tempers, arguments – with one of two added burdens. Either they won't have the foggiest idea what is going on; or they will know only too well and have to carry on the fiction of being 'protected' by you. All too often, the first time young people know something is deeply wrong in their family is when there is a dramatic upheaval – the family moves, they are told their parents are seeking a divorce, someone dies. Far from protecting them, keeping them in the dark makes the experience far worse. They seldom soldier on, blissfully unaware there are problems looming. Paul is now 17 and his parents separated when he was 15. He remembers:

❝I was 10 when I first realised my parents weren't happy. They always seemed to be either arguing or giving each other the silent treatment. It struck home because I had two friends I spent a lot of time with. Todd had really cool parents. I found it odd at first because they were always hugging each other and they went out, too – you know, to restaurants and such. My parents never went out as a couple and I don't think I can remember them ever kissing. John's parents were like mine, always sniping. Then John told us his Dad had left and there was going to be a divorce. I went home and looked at my family and I knew it was only a matter of time. And I was right. ❞

You may think silence buys them time to enjoy a worry-free period. In the event, it usually means they have those worries for just as long as if you had come clean; but they have them without the benefit of your support and understanding. You may feel that if your anxiety never materialises, keeping it from them will mean they never have to deal with the problem. What you will be forgetting is the power of a young person's imagination and fantasy. Simone found this out to her son, Jean-Paul's, cost.

❝When Jean-Paul was 13, we went through a bad spell with my husband's career. It looked as if he would be made redundant and we were terrified. We had a mortgage and I only had a part-time job. We didn't want to worry the children so we kept it quiet and went on as normal, or so we thought. Anyway, when he was around 14 or so, Jean-Paul started having problems at school and he was eventually excluded for a couple of weeks. We couldn't understand why he was acting this way. By that time, all the troubles with Bill's job had blown over and he had been promoted. Jean-Paul ended up seeing a therapist. It turned out much of the problem went back to that time when we were so worried and thinking we hid it so well from the kids. He had been convinced the family was going to break up and it was all his fault and all sorts of wild fancies. ❞

Family crises are one area that clearly do need to be discussed, however much you might think your young people aren't ready to handle the news. They may not be mature enough to make decisions or handle being in charge of the situation, but they are old enough to hear about it, have an opinion and have it heard. A family crisis, of whatever form and whatever magnitude, is an ideal subject for a Family Round Table, and for brainstorming.

The reason we often don't tell our teenagers, or our children at any age, when families disintegrate or family members are ill, distressed or about to die, may be twofold. We all suffer from the almost superstitious belief that giving a name to an event gives it reality. Acknowledge your marriage is in trouble, and it will collapse; say Gran is ill, and she will die; own up to the fact that Dad has problems, and he will have that breakdown. Don't mention it, and perhaps it will all go away. The other reason we keep quiet is because most of us have been brought up lacking the skills to deal with distress – our own or that of other people. We may feel we can't cope with our own anxieties; we certainly fear we won't be able to deal with theirs. We are scared our own misery will overwhelm us and we won't be able to deal with it. We are scared their misery will overwhelm us and we will be shown up, as bad and incompetent parents who can't 'fix it'. Our response to unhappiness, so often, is to believe that if we can sweep it under the carpet and forget about it, it will go away. It seldom does. Lumps under the carpet tend to shift around and trip you up at the most unexpected moments, as Simone found. A face-to-face talk with all the family, putting your cards on the table and giving them a chance to have their feelings brought out in the open, may be painful and the scene of tears, but it is better than the alternative. The points to keep in mind are these:

- If there is a crisis, ignoring it doesn't make it vanish.
- If tears are shed and distress expressed, your telling

them what the situation is hasn't made them have those anxieties – they would have been felt anyway. We often react with panic to the signs of sadness – 'Now look what you've done! You've made them cry!' – as if no tears means no hurt. On the contrary, no tears means no chance to resolve the problem, while bringing it out in the open is the first step to getting on top of it.

- When you keep quiet, you tell young people that you don't respect them, trust them or feel able to be open with them. As well as being upset about the area of secrecy itself, they have the added discomfort of having to come to terms with the fact that you lied to them.

Young people have more sense, strength and initiative than we often give them credit for. Share the situation with them and you may be pleasantly surprised at how much they may help you.

Family secrets

A knottier problem may be if, and how, to disclose secrets you may feel are not yours to discuss. Most families have a skeleton in their cupboard – a black sheep who is never mentioned, a tragedy that is never discussed. Perhaps there was a family member who committed a crime, or someone who killed themselves, or a relative who died from a disease such as cancer, and a tradition has developed not to talk about the subject.

Mary came to counselling because her husband had been getting steadily more depressed and desperate as his thirtieth birthday approached. She was both surprised and hurt by his total refusal to even discuss the possibility of a party, and his rage when he found out she was planning one as a surprise. The one clue she had was a remark by his mother, that, 'Of course, he's so like his father's older brother.' She had always thought his father had been the eldest in his family – and that all the others had been girls. It gradually emerged that when her husband had been 5 years old, his uncle had killed himself – on his thirtieth birthday. He'd been Godfather to Mary's husband and up until that time, everyone often remarked how much the boy had resembled his Uncle. Mary's husband never forgot this link, and the silence around the whole subject left him alone with his thoughts and fears on that tie. He had always thought that he was doomed to die at 30, as had his uncle, and as he drew nearer to his own thirtieth birthday, he became more depressed and frightened.

> Far from holding the matter at arms' length
> keeping family secrets gives them a power far beyond
> their real import

It's actually almost impossible to keep something from your own or your family's past entirely concealed. People talk – if only in veiled hints and muttered asides, that are always heard and eventually decoded. Even if you are the only one to know and you're not talking, the secret is likely to prey on your mind and affect the way you behave. This, in itself, often results in the one thing you fear coming to pass. When they have learned, or had some glimpse of, the mystery, not discussing it leaves young people to imagine the reasons for what happened, and why you won't mention it. Like Mary's husband, they may feel drawn to and connect with the hidden truth and doomed to repeat whatever it is you won't be open about. Or they feel responsible or criticised or tainted. Keeping secrets is always dangerous because the imagined truth is usually more painful and destructive than the real truth. Furthermore, what young people learn from the fact that you won't be honest with them is that you lie and cannot be trusted. The secret itself is likely to be less devastating than realising your parents themselves are unreliable and dishonest.

Family Round Tables can be an ideal time to bring up such subjects, to ask your kids what they might have heard, what they might have thought and how they might feel about any stories, and sorting them out. In the process, you may well find that you have made, and are carrying the burden of, assumptions that you could all be able to disperse.

Sandra's grandfather died while she was away at university, just before her finals. Her mother decided it would be better not to tell her, in case it affected her. When Sandra came home for the weekend at the end of her exams, she discovered the funeral had been held three days before. She went back to university and carried on as if nothing had happened. What she felt, however, was that she had never had the chance to say goodbye to him. Sandra had been the first girl from her family to go to college, and it had been her grandfather who had backed her up, against her own mother's apparent opposition. She felt that her mother had kept the old man's death from her out of spite, and because his concern for her had contributed to his ill-health. She never forgave either her mother or herself, and when her own children drew near to their GCSEs, she found herself discouraging them from thoughts of college.

Matt, Sandra's husband, called a Family Round Table and Sandra found herself telling the family about her feelings of never having said goodbye to the grandfather she loved, her anger towards her mother and her own guilt. The rest of the family – her son, daughter and her husband – were all able to share their memories and impressions about Sandra's own mother, and about the possibility of stress contributing to her grandfather's death. It emerged that Sandra's mother had never forgiven herself for what she quickly recognised as a mistake. Whether she had opposed Sandra's ambitions earlier, she was now overwhelmingly proud of her daughter's achievements – just unable to say so to her in the face of her cold hostility. She certainly told everyone else how pleased and admiring she was. And Matt remembered his mother-in-law once saying her father had died of pancreatic cancer – unlikely to be associated with stress.

Sandra had had good reason to be angry with her mother, but no reason to feel in any way responsible or even contributory to her grandfather's death. The family brainstormed how to lay the past to rest. They decided to hold a leave-taking ceremony to make up for the funeral she had missed all those years before. They all visited the cemetery and enacted their own small, informal funeral, and then had a wake where they talked about Sandra's grandfather, looked at photos of him and heard stories about him. Sandra wrote her mother a letter, telling her what they had done and why, explaining her anger and pain but saying she had now put it behind her – and she found she had.

Money matters

Money is also a subject young people say they would like to talk over in more detail. Young people would appreciate being involved in discussions about family finances. Money – your income, their allowance – often form the core of arguments, but teenagers' irresponsibility about cash can frequently be traced to the fact that they are not given, and not asked to have, a say in money management. It's no good telling young people money doesn't grow on trees if you don't let them have an insight into where it does come from, how it may be earned and how they may contribute.

A common disagreement is teens' partiality for leaving lights on all over the house. If yours do this and you find yourself forever complaining about electricity bills, one way of dealing with it is to let them see and understand how much the bill is and what sort of budget it has to be paid out of. You could offer them a productivity deal. If next year's bill is reduced, you'll make them a percentage payment from the difference between the last one and the next. The higher the reduction, the more they get. If the bill stays the same or goes up, the difference comes out of their allowance. Their behaviour may change when they have as much at stake in the outcome as you do. Children need to learn how to budget, and

---

Exercise: **money management**

Ask everyone in the household to keep a log for a month, listing ALL money in and out. When you are keeping track, it can be hard to be frank. The temptation is either to leave some elements off the list or to stop yourself buying certain items you feel might be extravagant. You won't learn if you aren't honest. After a month, bring the lists to a Family Round Table, with the following agreement: there is to be no criticism of people for their spending. What you are there to look at is what is spent on what, and whether you could be more efficient. What needs to be understood is that everyone is entitled to a fair share, and that people should have the right to decide what they do with their own money. Just because you feel buying such-and-such would be wasted on you doesn't mean it is a waste for the person who did buy it.

However, being responsible for your own cash also means being responsible for your own choice as to what to do with it. Your teens have every right to blow an entire month's allowance on a new video game or whatever, if that's what they really want, just as you have the choice to spend a significant sum from the budget on going to Florida for a summer holiday or buying cigarettes. As long as they realise that, just as you have to live with your decisions, so do they. Which means you won't bail them out of experiencing the consequences. If you fork out, on top of their usual pocket money or whatever you call it, to pay for clothes, fares or entertainment when it's their lack of foresight that has got them in trouble, they'll never learn. But similarly, if you carp at the choices they make while not allowing them the opportunity to do the same on your spending, they'll never learn to be discriminating and to trust their own tastes.

the earlier you pass on these skills, the better. And if the real problem is that you don't feel confident in your own financial control, make teaching them an opportunity for everyone to brush up on skills.

When you discuss, and especially when you argue over, money, it's worth considering and talking about its significance other than being the coin of the realm. Money is about worth, and in our society it has become the way we value each other. Arguments over money are often really about care and attention, about being valued. We may ask for a raise at work because we want or need an increase in income but we may also ask for it because we'd like to know whether the people we work for appreciate what a good job we're doing. When children ask their parents for money, or new clothes, shoes, games, computers, what they are often really asking is, 'Do you love me, do you care about me, do you rate me?' The more love, time, affection and attention you give your teenagers, the less they may need the trappings.

Happy holidays

Holidays can be a particular bone of contention in many families. Young people feel strongly that their wishes are not considered when it comes to planning where, when and for how long holidays are taken. Adults often feel that they deserve to pick what is done – they're the ones who need a rest after working hard. Parents also often feel that if they did give their teens a say, disagreements wouldn't be any less. Says Brian:

❛We tried it two years ago. We told our three that they could choose where we went, because they said they all had a horrible time the previous year. I don't remember it being so awful. We had the usual moans and sulks but no more than usual and they also seemed to have a largely good holiday. Anyway, we told them to get the brochures, and after three

weeks of reminding them I finally went and got them. So
they moaned that I hadn't found anything worthwhile. I
said they had one more week to get down and fetch what
they wanted or we'd choose. So then we had two weeks of
their wrangling among themselves and the eldest finally
said they'd decided. They chose an all-in hotel in the Med.
It was OK, in some ways, but there was nothing else for
miles so when we'd all got bored of the facilities and what
was on offer at the hotel, there was nothing else to do and
nowhere else to go. And then they blamed each other for
the choice and blamed us for letting them do it. So last year
we went back to making the arrangements and I suppose
there was just as much disagreement, but at least we got
what we wanted. I told them it's only a few more years until
they can bloody well pay for their own holidays and do what
they want! **❯**

If, instead of handing over total responsibility to one section of the family, all of you brainstormed what you
might want, you could come up with a solution that suited everyone, with fewer feelings of resentment. What
often gets left out in thinking about holidays is a consideration of what goes to make up the perfect break for
each individual. Some people look to relaxation – lazing
on a beach. Others feel better for exercise, activity
and/or exploration. Some don't feel they've had a satisfying trip unless they get a suntan, others see meeting
new people, eating new foods or seeing new sights as the
proof of a good time. An honest examination of what
every person needs can help you build up a profile of
what sort of holiday you might want to construct. But it's
no good doing this for your teens – you need to do it
with them. What upsets young people is not just spending time on holiday doing things they don't want to do.
It's being dragged around, never having been asked what
they'd like, being told it's all for their benefit and feeling
powerless. There's nothing quite as conducive to a temper tantrum as being told to be grateful for something

you don't want and aren't enjoying! Once you've been consulted and made a part of the decision-making, anyone can put up with a percentage of time spent pleasing other members of the party – as long as you know your favourite bit is on the schedule somewhere, sometime. Having choice also allows people, young or mature, to give something they might not have thought they'd like a chance. Once you can see on paper what you have to cram in to suit everyone, you can ask a travel specialist to suggest something that fits all your needs and your budget.

Paula and her sons Adam and Joe tried this as a method.

❝I love trailing round old churches and going to local markets. Being a single parent I was always a bit possessive – I felt I had to keep the boys with me, to make sure they were behaving themselves. And our life at home seems so full and busy, that I felt if we didn't spend free time together on holiday, we would never have that so-called "quality time" together. It took me a long time to realise that all those sulks and arguments were hardly quality. Having talked to other Mums, I tried the brainstorming technique. We all came up with a plan that involved staying with some friends at a villa, and dividing up our time into sections. It sounds a bit regimental but it really worked. We had some days when we all went off and did our own thing. I got my markets, my churches and my sunbathing. They got canoeing, mountain biking and white water rafting. But then, one day I joined them for a long walk and they came wandering round a lovely castle with me, so we each did something we might have grumbled about but because it was just for a part of the holiday, it was fun. When we were together, we had so much to talk about it was really wonderful and we enjoyed each others' company so much more. ❞

Home style

Young people also want to discuss and be involved in the day-to-day arrangements in what is, after all, their home too. We pay the rent so we tend to feel that running the home is our field. Some parents may be happy to let their kids decide decoration in their own rooms and hand over decision-making for their own schedule to their youngsters, but many of us wouldn't think to involve them in wider or more general discussions. This may be one reason for the common arguments we have over tidiness. If they don't feel that this is their territory as much as yours, they may feel very little incentive to keep it looking good. Clothes and belongings scattered around serve another function, too. Just as animals scent mark in territory they want to take over, kids drop mess wherever they go to make an imprint and say 'This is MINE'. If they feel the living room is just as much their territory as yours, they may feel less driven to stake a claim in ways that drive you wild. One way of making the point that we all should be contributing in some way to the smooth working of your family is by sharing chores around the home.

Chores and sharing the load can be a focus for rows. If young people feel that they're having jobs dumped on them just because you're being mean, they may skimp and avoid them and that leads to you getting angry. The fact is that young people do have a busy time of it – they tend to have almost every moment at school organised and full, and they may look at home as a refuge from endless instruction and involvement. But most young people are also fair-minded. Again, if shown just exactly what you do during the day and what it takes to keep everyone in clean clothes and fish-fingers, they are often more than happy to take their share.

Exercise: **Team Chore Chart**

To make the every-day running of your home easier, convene Family Round Table and brainstorm what needs to be done. With your young people draw up a Team Chore Chart. Discuss all the chores that need to be done and list them on a chart. Discuss how and by when each task needs to be completed. Then talk over a 'weighting' for each chore. That is, some might be light and easy, some dirty and difficult. Some may be fun to do and others disliked by everyone. Once you've got your weightings, you can begin talking over distribution.

Certain members of the family may put themselves down for certain jobs to be permanently theirs, while other tasks can be taken turn and turn about. Or you may all decide that all jobs are done in a rotation. All members of the family – parents and any other adult living or staying with you – should be an equal part of this scheme. Once it's been drawn up and agreed, all members should sign a contract. This means you all promise to keep the agreement and do your chores, to an agreed standard and by an agreed time each week, day or month. If there are any difficulties, you can call another Family Round Table to talk it over.

S*E*X and drugs and rock and roll

Family matters are felt to be the most important by many young people, but the more controversial issues are the ones they often feel get left out. Young people think adults frequently fudge discussing moral subjects with them, fobbing them off with excuses such as they're too young or it's too complicated to explain. The issues they would really like to talk about include whether it is ever right to steal or lie, abuse and bullying, drugs, and the hottest potato of all – S*E*X. They want to know about attitudes and beliefs, about gender and homosexuality and, most of all, what sex is actually like.

We tend to parcel this particular subject away, calling it The Facts of Life. Our treatment of it actually separates it from normal life, making it an issue and a world apart. Sex is, of course, something that does occupy a locked off compartment in our lives sometimes – the times when it is going badly. When we have happy, relaxed, comfortable sexual relationships, sex forms a foundation and a background. Like the sound of a running stream, it's there. You notice and enjoy it but it can fade comfortably into the scenery and only comes into focus when you want it to. When sex is a problem, it grates. You're always aware of it, but constantly want to avert your eyes and ignore it's existence.

Our attitude to sex actually makes it a problem, which is sad for us and sad for our kids. You don't really have any choice about whether to give sex education to your kids – only about the type. There is, of course, a distinction between being open about the subject and the issues; in other words, being open about your feelings and the theory, and talking about what you and they actually DO. Neither parents nor young people should be disclosing the intimate details of their own sex lives to each other. You shouldn't fear you have to or expect that they must. Being open about the subject most certainly doesn't mean overstepping the bounds of privacy and respect. But our own, natural, unease and embarrassment about discussing our sex lives is what is often behind our difficulties in talking easily about sex with our young people. We feel embarrassed about our ignorance or shy about our perceived failures. When they ask us questions, instead of being able to say, 'I don't know, even though you and I might expect me to be an expert in this area!' it is all too easy to tell them off for asking such a disgusting question, and accuse them of being sexual degenerates and perverts for even thinking about such matters! The anger is really at being, as we see it, 'caught out', at not knowing or not being comfortable with a subject we feel we should have down pat. The anger is with ourselves, but we dump it on them.

Sex should be about pleasure

Our attitude towards sex and sexuality in this culture tends to be one of unease and disease. We see sex as much more to do with risk, problems and difficulties than about joy, enjoyment and pleasure. Our over-riding concern, then, when we face the fact that our teens are approaching an age when they may be considering sexual activity, is that they may be getting into danger. A large part of this viewpoint has been set by what we see their growing up means to us. We do tend to pigeon-hole people in this society. We consider that active sexuality is seen as appropriate to a specific time in our adult life. You have to be old enough, but not too old, to be neither jumping the gun nor being dirty old people.

When your teens cross from being children to being sexually active, that can be seen as bumping you from the 'Still young enough to do it' category into the 'Old enough to know better' group. You don't want them to grow up. It means they are about to leave you and no longer need you; it means they are about to invest their love and attention in people other than you, to find a partner who will be first in their hearts; and it means you will have to take on the mantle of sexually inactive tribal elder!

We dress up these somewhat selfish and unworthy fears in something far more high-minded and generous, as fears and worries about their health, their morals, their safety. All of which may be real – but only if you can first separate them from what may be the greatest fear; that it's you who are getting old.

Because we see sex as a dark, frightening and dangerous activity, we see their becoming involved in sexual activity as the signal for often overwhelming anxiety. This means that we usually confuse two elements, which are sexuality and sexual activity. What your teenager usually wants you to help them with is the exploration and defining of their sexuality. Since you are scared that doing this may trigger them to become involved in sexual activity at too young an age, you try to suppress or control behaviour by suppressing or controlling discussion. But allowing and encouraging someone to become aware of and be at home with their sexuality is not the same as condoning their having sex.

Being aware of our own sexuality

Being comfortable with our sexuality is not the same as being in a sexual relationship or as being sexually active. Indeed, for some people, being truly at home in their own sexual feelings is to be celibate. Awareness of sexuality is a part of coming to terms with yourself as a complete, creative and happy human being, whether that means you are sexually active or not, sexually partnered or not, and whether it's men or women to whom you are attracted. Being at home with your sexuality means you can openly acknowledge and feel comfortable with having sexual feelings and knowing you can enjoy them. It means being in control of your own sexual desires and neither abusing nor misusing them nor allowing anybody else to do so. It means being picky about how you express your sexual feelings, only sharing them with people you care deeply about and respect.

Most parents fear that acknowledging their teens' sexuality will be like unlocking a Pandora's box, letting out all sorts of uncontrollable and destructive feelings and behaviours. In my experience, it is the opposite. Trying to keep the box locked is what makes it boil over and explode. Trying to suppress young people's self-awareness is what makes sex such a fascinating and then destructive subject, forcing them to find out about it in snatched and furtive ways. And when you have to explore a subject in a sly, underhand manner, it taints the subject itself, making it similarly sly and underhand, nasty and potentially hurtful.

Young people want to talk about sex. They want to discuss the emotional ramifications – the way they feel about the adults in their lives who are important to them and the way growing feelings for their peers overshadows this. They want at first to talk about their feelings for role models – pop/rock and movie stars or other people they admire. When they move on from these early infatuations they want to talk about the feelings they have for people they know.

If we react with laughter or scorn, by teasing or putting them down; if we criticise or reject them or their concerns, our teens soon learn. They learn that they or their feelings are unacceptable and that you are not the right person to approach about these matters. They also want to talk about the practical and physical aspects – about body changes during puberty and during sexual excitement, about what happens when you become aroused, what happens during sexual activity and what sex feels like. They don't necessarily want to have these conversations with you – the taboo against discussing the intimate details with family members is a real and vital one. But they need to have them with someone and they need your permission to do so. Permission is given by your letting them know that:

- Such subjects are allowable and appropriate
- They are acceptable if they ask about these things
- You won't be hurt if they go elsewhere for a listening ear and answers.

Young people should be able to express their sexuality. This doesn't mean we need to condone or encourage any or all levels of sexual activity or expression. We need to see, and help them to see, sexual expression as a journey and a range of behaviour and manifestations. It ranges from a simple awareness of self right through to complex relationships with full sexual activity. If we don't feel they are ready to make the full journey yet, that's fine – but we do need to accept that before anyone goes the whole way, they need to take a first step. The first step a child takes is stumbling and hesitant but they improve as we applaud, guide and encourage. If a teenager's first step into sexual awareness is hedged about with guilt, fear, self-doubt and disgust, they are more likely to grab experiences as a way of trying to feel better about themselves.

They are likely to be defiant, secretive and miserable. The more we encourage and are positive, the more they are likely to be open, caring and relaxed. They are also more likely to wait. In countries such as the Netherlands, young people do benefit from a far more pragmatic attitude to sex and sexuality and they receive a more enlightened sex education than we do. The result is that their young people have their first experience of sex at a far later age than those in the UK, USA and other western countries. Being more up-front and open about sex and sexuality would be important, if only to get them to delay sexual exploration until they are older. A far more valuable reason is that many of the problems in our lives can be traced to the poor self-image and lack of self-esteem that comes about when sex and sexual knowledge have been dealt with badly when we were young.

So what, exactly, you talk about is less important than the fact that you are willing to talk at all. The key is to remember that:

- You don't have to know all the facts
- You don't have to be an expert red hot lover to be able to talk about sex
- You don't have to be comfortable and unembarrassed to start with.

It's fine to admit lack of information and to say, 'I don't know, let's look it up and find out.' Most of the time, however, your fear of being shown up won't even materialise. This is because what young people want to talk about isn't the facts but their feelings – and feelings and opinions are something everyone has and is entitled to. It's also OK to admit to inexperience. It's obviously true that we tend to value expertise and competence in this society, but we also have a sneaking admiration for the person who cheerfully says they can't do everything. If we're feeling lacking in skills and a person we look up to says they're in the same boat, far from despising them we greet the disclosure with a certain amount of relief. It means there is hope for us, as well! This means that it can actually help your teens, and help all of you gain skills, if you can say, 'Well, I'm not too sure about that either so let's get better at it at the same time.' And most important of all, the best way to deal with unease and shyness about sexual matters in yourself and your teens is to face up to it, admit it and work through it. 'This makes me really embarrassed, but that's because nobody ever talked to me properly about it when I was young, so let's do better, shall we?' As with so many subjects, you may need to accept that when you actually talk and what you actually talk about should be in your teenagers' hands, not yours. They'll clam up if you try to force the pace and pick the time. But they'll come to you if they have every reason to expect you to be willing to listen and to be honest. They won't come to you if they know you're going to be inflexible, judgmental, unaccepting and dismissive.

There are several spin-offs from being able to talk about sex with your teens. One, as already mentioned, is the likelihood of their delaying sexual exploration until they are ready to deal with it maturely. Another is that when they do, they are likely to use safer sex practices, protecting themselves and their partners against pregnancy and sexual infection. Another is that they are far more likely to keep safe in other ways. Young people who can talk honestly and with trust to the adults who care for them are less at risk of being involved in sexual abuse – as the target of such behaviour or the abuser. The sort of self-confidence and awareness of self-worth that goes with being able to talk frankly shields young people against bullying and harassment, sexual or otherwise, and helps them know how to deal with it, if it does arise. The main drawback about being made to feel guilty, inadequate and wrong – all consequences of sexual ignorance and sexual silence – is that when bad stuff happens, you feel it's your fault and you deserved it. Our teens deserve better of us.

Drink and drugs

Every parent's nightmare is to find out that their children have been experimenting with substances, whether cannabis, solvents or Ecstasy. To a lesser degree, we dread finding out they have tried alcohol or tobacco, but we reserve our greatest fears for the illegal drugs. We tend to feel that drugs are a one-way trip to disaster and death. Even a pregnancy, we think, is more recoverable. We certainly feel every teen is at risk from being offered illegal drugs and that once tried, the situation can never be salvaged.

How we deal with drugs in this society is guaranteed to both confuse and irritate most young people. You have only to look around you to realise that most of us use drugs of some sort or other, at some time or other. We take drugs for medical conditions, to treat illness or stop discomfort. Some of these drugs have effects that give them a use beyond the therapeutic and into the recreational. We also have substances that are purely used for their pleasant effect. Every society has substances or behaviour that is used to make people feel different.

Some cultures use fermented, distilled or otherwise processed foodstuffs or drinks – drinks made from yak milk, grain, fruit or vegetables, or dried mushrooms. Others burn various leaves or the resin made from the sap of flowers or trees. Other cultures have found that hyperventilating or depriving their bodies of oxygen by chanting, singing or holding their breath, has the same effect. Others discover that whirling around or dancing causes dizziness and others that fasting or starving can make you feel euphoric too. All of these activities have certain things in common. They can make you feel good, give you the impression that you are 'out of yourself', and when taken in the company of other people, will ease tension and make you feel sociable, in tune and close to the people with whom you share the experience.

> Every single culture has some form of mind-altering substance or behaviour

The only variable is whether these substances or behaviours are ultimately harmful in themselves. Anything, if used to the exclusion of learning proper social skills and if allowed to become obsessive, will be injurious. The only question is, 'Is this going to be destructive of itself, or does the taking of it bring the user into dangerous waters?' The fact is that the substances we use legally in our society are dangerous in the extreme. Far more people die prematurely because of nicotine addiction and from the effects of alcohol than from the use of cannabis or Ecstasy. So when we come down heavily on teenagers about the sorts of drugs they may be offered, we risk having them ignore anything we might say by missing many of the contradictions in our own attitudes. What young people want to talk to you about, then, is what makes something a drug – how it works, why we use it, how it affects us and what are the problems. Simply telling them the stuff is dangerous and shouldn't be used won't stop them.

Why do we use drugs?

Young people try drugs for all sorts of reasons – probably the same reasons most older people go on using them. One may be that they do believe that they are immortal and invulnerable. 'It'll never happen to me' is the teenager's motto. They need to push the boundaries of risk to see how far they can go, and flying in the face of your warnings is one way of doing so. If you tell a small child that the one thing they shouldn't do is push beans up their nose, the next thing you will find is that they've shoved a whole sack up there. Tell a teenager drugs are dangerous and deadly, and they'll dive straight in. Young people use drugs to show off. Or to belong to one group – their friends – or to separate themselves from another – you and their family. Or they use them to feel better about themselves, to deal with pressures and drown out anxieties. If we only talk about the horror stories, we make it difficult, if not impossible, to discuss this subject with them. Telling them that drugs can only addict and destroy them – and will make them feel terrible – doesn't open the lines of communication. The problem is that if this is true, why do so many people use them?

We often don't dare consider the truth, which is that people use drugs because they can make you feel good, because we're terrified such an admission would send them hot-footing it straight to the nearest friendly, neighbourhood drug dealer. Just as with sex, we fear that not condemning is the same as condoning or encouraging. This may work as an approach IF, and only if, they were never, ever going to be in the position of having access to a drug. This is simply impossible. Drugs aren't only the illegal stuff you inject into your veins. We're talking here about items you can buy over the counter perfectly legally, those you can be given by your own GP and then pass on, as well as those that can only be bought on the wrong side of the law. But these days, illegal and even dangerous substances are available in most pubs, in most towns.

If your teenagers meet someone who offers them 'a taste', or see their friends doing so, and it doesn't harm them, it doesn't kill them and it does feel good – what you have told them is going to come into question. If you only told them the dark side and the dark side doesn't emerge, they'll add one and one and conclude you were lying, or didn't know what you were talking about. And then nothing of what you said or will say will be worth remembering. If you don't discuss the whole package, you risk having the essential bits thrown out with the nonsense. It's perfectly possible, for instance, to say that some drugs make you feel fantastic – better than sex, better than anything they might feel before or after – and yet that you have no intention of ever trying it. It's far better for them to hear the upside if you want them to pay attention to the downside – which is that short-term pleasure is followed by long-term trouble.

But the most important aspect young people probably want to discuss is why the drugs our society feels are acceptable, such as nicotine and alcohol, are so different to the ones we feel are dangerous. Is a joint so much worse than a stiff G&T or a fag? Have you never tried anything illegal such as cannabis or pills? They need to talk over why illegality might make a drug far more tempting than if it were readily available – which is why the whole mystique and paraphernalia of injecting seems so much more exiting than queuing up for a methadone prescription. And the perils of being pulled in by people who might want to have them graduate from one relatively soft drug to another far more addictive one, which is why smoking marijuana may indeed lead on to other things.

The only way you are going to get your teens to listen to your fears, is if you are prepared to listen to their thoughts, questions and criticisms. And why acceptance and tolerance are far more powerful than rules and prohibition. Young people who feel confident and loved are far less likely to dabble, and if they do so, experiment with the substances that are less risky, in a less risky way.

The emotional stuff

Young people want to talk about emotional issues. They want to talk about and explore a wide range of feelings, but particularly those associated with love, attraction and friendship. As a society, we deal with developing emotional literacy – understanding feelings and being comfortable with experiencing, discussing and expressing them – very badly. The continuing legacy of the British Stiff Upper Lip means that many of us feel acutely ill at ease with emotions. We often want to shield our young people from the dangers of the real world, from anger and rejection, from loss and failure, from disillusionment and disappointment. But you can't live your youngsters' lives for them. If they don't have the experience themselves, they don't learn from it and, most importantly, you don't have to protect kids from feelings.

What you can, and should, do is give them protection in the form of support. If they know you will always be there for them, they can cope with more than you might imagine. If you've brought them up to feel good about themselves, they will be able to weather most setbacks. If you tell them you love them often enough, not only will they believe it and know they can come to you for help but they will believe they are loveable and worthwhile. Whatever then happens, they will have hope and the sense that they will live to succeed another day. It's therefore important to talk as often as possible, using the magic words 'I feel . . .'. The more they hear you being honest and frank about your feelings, the easier it will be for them to do so too.

Life, The Universe and Everything

Adolescence is the one (and probably the only) time in your life when it is possible to be intense and fascinated about Life, The Universe and Everything without being a hippy, a quantum mechanic, or feeling foolish. Teenagers really do want to thrash out the big, philosophical issues – why are we here, why is there war, why can't everyone just love each other? Don't laugh, don't sneer and don't point out that you went through all that too and nothing much has changed in the intervening years. For a start, world-shattering advances in science, mathematics, medicine, philosophy and literature will, usually, have had their beginnings in a teenage discussion. If you shame them into shutting up you will never know what you might have nipped in the bud – a cure for cancer or final proof of some obscure mathematical theorem.

The main point is that everyone creates their set of beliefs to live by in these sessions – a moral code, a philosophy. When we talk about the universe, what we're often working towards is our own place within it. Tell teenagers that they are unimportant and that their thoughts are hackneyed, imitative and boring, and where will they find a belief in themselves? What they may do, of course, is fall prey to the first person with a strong sense of self-belief who tells them what to think, feel and believe – which is where abusive relationships and cults may come in to their lives. Who knows – you may find the fun and excitement once again in thinking about less mundane matters than whether you have enough soap powder to see you through to Thursday.

Current affairs

Young people are also far more interested in what goes on in the world than we often credit them for being and want to keep up with current affairs. If they seem bored or turned off by newspapers or the news, it's often because of the way these are presented or the way we discuss such matters in front of them. Given the opportunity to talk these subjects over with their parents or other adults, most teens want to discuss such matters and are far more clear-thinking than you might expect.

Forward to the future

Young people want to talk to you about the future – their own as well as the world's. They want to discuss education and what they may do with their lives, what they may make of themselves. Just because they change their ambitions and interests from one day to the next does not mean they are flighty or insincere or incapable of choosing for themselves – simply that there are so many possibilities and it takes time to decide.

Indeed, one major difference between their world and ours may be the fact that change will be valued more than stability and people will be encouraged and able to flit from one job to another, one profession to another far more easily. In this, perhaps more than any other aspect, young people need you to listen and respect them and their opinions, for them to feel able to open up and talk to you – and for them then to be able to listen to you. Your teens will want to talk to you about what to do when you favour homework and they want television, you think they should be rocket scientists and they want to be eco-warriors. If you don't dismiss what they feel is important they are far less likely to ignore what you think is vital. It is worth listening to them and negotiating a middle line. When young people seem bored, disaffected, lazy and disinclined to consider a future, there is usually a reason, which you are only going to hear if you pay attention. They may really be depressed by what they have heard in the news about the way their world is going. They may be depressed or frightened about what they see is happening in their own family, their own life. Finding it difficult to face up to their own anxieties, they may be retreating into the pose of, 'There's no point in talking to you/doing anything/getting qualifications – you don't listen/what's the point?/there aren't going to be any jobs, anyway!' A young person who refuses to move forward and look to a future may be saying that there is something changing in their life they find alarming or saddening. They may be unable to stop the arguments in the home, the loss of a friend or the loss of that certainty children have that their parents know everything and will always 'make it right'. But what they can do is dig in their heels and say, 'I'm not shifting – so there!' The only way you will be able to help them see they can make a difference to their own lives is by hearing their feelings and giving them the right to express them.

Personal issues

Teens want to talk to you about personal issues – their own hobbies and their private life away from you, their friends and other influences. Friends are often a major issue in houses where there are teenagers. You hate them, they love them – and the more you object, criticise and carp, the more they may cling to that outsider. You may find yourself focusing on their manners, their clothes, their behaviour, their musical tastes, their background, their ambitions (or, more usually, lack of), their appearance. It's truly amazing how many young people have friends that are 'a bad influence'. After all, if we listened to ourselves and did a little simple arithmetic we'd soon realise that there are more bad influences around than hot dinners – so how come we haven't descended into total barbarism? And who are these 'bad influences' that the parents of our children's friends complain about? The truth is that their friends often become the scapegoat for all the things a parent dislikes about their own teens' attitudes and lifestyles. And, of course, the very worst crime their friends commit is that they take your babies away from you!

Charting a course through these shark-infested waters may mean resisting projecting your anxieties and fears about the loss of your children onto other people. Your kids are growing up, and the straight choice we have is to celebrate and enjoy this change – or resist and mourn it. If you take a long, hard look at your teens' friends, you are likely to find there is usually very little to differentiate them from your own.

When young people want to draw that line that says, 'I'm different from the adults and the same as my friends', the way they do it is usually by their appearance – their clothes, hair and make-up and, more recently, other additions such as body-piercing and tattoos. Even young children can have their own ideas about their personal style which you may find offensive. Teens make a science of finding something that makes you wince – which is, of course, the whole point of it. Any argument that 'It's tarty, wild, disgusting, rebellious, dangerous and stereotypes you as such' will fall on deaf ears – not least because the response may well be, 'Doh – yeah, that's what it's supposed to do!' Underneath the wacky paint, wild fashions and crazy hair style is the same person you gave birth to.

Their parents – your feelings, past and life

Last, but by no means least, young people want to talk about you. They want to hear about your past – your childhood, your growing up – and indeed your present

and future. They want to hear the truth about your past –
not a sanitised version that insists you never wore clothes
your parents hated, never played truant, never inhaled.

❝I was 15 before I found out my Dad had been married
before he married my Mum. It was my aunt who let slip that
titbit, just in passing. She was staggered I didn't know and
when I asked her to tell me more, she then clamed up and
said I'd have to talk to them. It was three years before I did,
and then it was in the middle of a blazing row. Looking
back, I now know that my aunt's revelation wasn't too much
of a surprise but it was a turning point because it made me
feel I couldn't trust them or talk to them. After all, if they'd
keep something so important from their lives a secret, what
else were they keeping from me, and why should I be honest with them if they couldn't be with me? But I had felt
there was something they would never talk about and I was
right.

'The row was because we'd been getting these weird
phone calls and them someone came to our house, and I
wanted to know who it was and they wouldn't tell me. Guess
what? I had a brother, and it was him. Well, a half brother,
but since I was an only child I did sort of think I had a right
to know about this. That was ten years ago. My brother and
I get on quite well, considering the fact that he had grown
up hating my Mum for taking his Dad away, and rather
blamed me as well when we first met. He's a really nice guy
so he's got over that. But I don't talk to my Dad much, and
when I do see my Mum it's rather strained. But they've only
themselves to blame for that, haven't they?❞

Your teens want to know how you grew up, how you got
on with your parents, what you wanted out of life and
whether you feel sad, happy, fulfilled or frustrated. We
do, so often, try to pass on the legacy of our own hopes
and dreams to our children. If we've unfulfilled ambitions, we frequently would like to inspire them to do
better – or to do it for us. If we've made mistakes, we
want to ensure they won't fall into the same traps. But

our methods of transmitting this wisdom are mostly by hint and concealed pressure; by lecture and warning. If you tell your young people about your own experiences, and let them make any connection that needs to be made, you are far more likely to have lessons learned. As far as they can be learned, that is. Because the hard truth for a parent to accept is that their children do have to make their own decisions, choices and mistakes and it may be impossible to prevent another human being from going their own way. And undesirable, too; the best knowledge comes from the discoveries we make ourselves. Talking to our young people about our own feelings and dreams is the best way of doing it.

Final word

Perhaps the final aim of this book is to enable your children to say of you what author Mark Twain once wrote:

‘When I was a boy of fourteen my father was so ignorant I could hardly stand to have the old man around. But when I got to be twenty-one I was astonished at how much he had learned in seven years. ’